Sarah

Bound by Addiction, Freed by Christ

SANDRA L. ROBINSON

MINDSTIR MEDIA

Published by Mindstir Media, LLC
45 Lafayette Rd | Suite 181| North Hampton, NH 03862 | USA
1.800.767.0531 | www.mindstirmedia.com

Printed in the United States of America
ISBN-13: 978-1-960142-97-9 (paperback)

Contents

Acknowledgements

A special thank you to Sarah for sharing her wisdom and love from beyond the grave. This is her legacy. Thank you to my husband, Luther, who loved us and held us together through thick and thin. Thank you to my family who faithfully and prayerfully stood by all three of us. There is no greater love. A special thank you for my friends, church family and prayer warriors too numerous to name. You are a powerful group of saints who always knew that God would get the last word. I love you! Thank you.

To my editors, you humble me with your talent and time. You helped formulate many jumbled thoughts into cohesive and meaningful pages. I couldn't have done it without you (I know you're nodding in agreement).

And finally, I thank the Lord, my Rock and Redeemer. May You be glorified by this work.

Introduction

September 19, 2019

'I Glitterly Can't.' So catchy and clever but this is precisely how I feel today.'

Ten months after writing that entry in her diary, my beautiful Sarah Louise Gangell overdosed and died at the age of 25.

"I Glitterly Can't" was the title of a pink sparkly notebook I had gifted Sarah. I knew pink and sparkly would make her laugh…or at least smile. As a child, Sarah scorned the color pink and refused to wear anything with sparkles. Still, every year I would buy her something pink or sparkly (or both!), knowing that her response would be a prolonged, "Mooooooooom" followed by an eye roll and our combined laughter. Somehow, in her early 20's, pink and sparkly became her go-to wardrobe preference. The journal was perfect; life was not.

Sarah's depression was once again drowning out hope. Addiction was waiting to pounce despite her being actively engaged in treatment for depression, heroin and other drug addictions. My daughter was entering her 43rd recovery placement in ten years. Through it all, journaling was a constant for Sarah and it was not uncommon to find her writing in two or more journals simultaneously. During these hard years, Sarah and I dreamed of writing a book for believers that shared our mutual—and mutually exclusive—experiences of living with her depression and addiction. When she was clean, we scribbled down chapter ideas and discussed content. Each chapter was to include both of our thoughts and words and be followed by thought-provoking questions, scriptures and music on which to meditate (music was a constant for Sarah). Each time we came close to writing the book, addiction came closer.

She took her last breath on July 13, 2020 in a lovely home, in a beautiful city, with a good job and great friends. What she left behind were detailed journals and countless letters addressed to me. Her writings ran the gamut from drama with friends to legal problems, to recovery placements or jail, to prayers, to gratitude lists and to the occasional "to-do" lists. But mostly the pages, like the ones in the glittery pink journal, held the outpourings of a girl who loved the Lord and lived in torment and spiritual warfare. Tormented by depression. Tormented by addiction. Tormented by their companions of guilt and shame.

In the following pages, I do my best to honor the plan. I try to tell our story from both sides through my reflections and Sarah's unedited journal entries and letters shown in italics. While Sarah carried much guilt and shame, she never shied from the ugly truth if it meant helping someone else. To that end, I think she would be very pleased with this book, seeing it—as I do—as a personal gift to those whose loved ones have and will wander from their paths. Our story is honest, raw and—I hope—encouraging.

May the Lord bless you as you share our journey and as you travel yours.

Chapter 1

Sandi and Sarah 101

"The Lord will fight for you; you need only be still."
Exodus 14:14 (NIV)

November 11, 2015

Hi Mom,

It's me. You're in Florida right now but I can't sleep and you're on my mind and you won't be back for 2 more weeks! So I will write you this nifty letter for when you get back. So also I don't forget what I was thinking about.

So I submitted my life story to my counselor which means I will have to read it to you and Luth @ some point. That's cool, and it's probably nothing you all don't know. I just wanted to get out on paper to you some thoughts about my childhood. The way you raised me—that couldn't have anything to do with how dad turned out and hurt you could it? Or even if it was just for my own spiritual well-being. You see, I always really resented you for being so "strict" on me and not allowing me to do what the "other kids did." Now obviously I don't, and honestly I don't even know if I was overprotected or just too dramatic. Probably a combo of both.

I never fit in 100% with the church crowd, and I never fit in 100% with the "others." (Which I so dearly wanted to fit in with the others) So, I think I was always angry with you b/c I thought you somehow outcasted me. Honestly, I got made fun of a lot for not having a button nose or perfect skin, and that obviously only added to my bitterness and hurt. Not to mention on some level of subconscious I probably felt abandoned by dad. Being outcast and different @ that time was so painful mom. I don't really think I ever told you how much I hurt. I was just a kid trying to fit into a hole of which I wasn't shaped for. Instead of trying to find a different hole, I kept trying to morph my peg to fit into that same space.

I got older and way less awkward looking. I still don't have the best self-esteem, but I do know that many people find me attractive and I do know I have a killer personality. The hurt has really lessened as I try now to embrace myself rather than deny my identity.

Anyways we watched a movie here, a little bit ago, called I think "For One More Day" or something. The mother came back to life to spend one last day with her alcoholic son and share some things he never understood about his childhood and things he resented her for. At one point, she leads her son to an old tree, which was engraved with the word, "please." She said she was married for years and still couldn't have a child. She wanted a baby so bad and was distraught. She carved the word, "please" into a tree to beg for a child. At the end of the scene, she explains that he was desperately wanted even years before conception.

That so reminded me of you and when you would tell me the story of how you marked the right days off on the calendar and well I guess for lack of better terms had to seduce my father and all this extra work just to have me. When I made *the connection in my mind that someone (you) went through all that work and probably painful knowledge that I have a feeling you might've known or at least suspected you would be a single mother. The fact that you did that just because you wanted to have ME is overwhelming mom. Like, Holy **** I was wanted and loved way before conception. (Obviously by God, but here I'm talkin' human love)*

Humans are ugly to each other, even parents to children and vice versa. I've come to the amazing realization recently of how much I'm loved. It's crazy and kind of stressful b/c pretty much I've been average, and I've been a disappointment. You obv say, "NO!" But that's the way I see it so, don't even argue. LOL.

It would seem great sometimes to take the easy way out the rest of my life. Sticking a needle in my arm seems like a freaking relief and breath of fresh air right now. But I have come to the sometimes-unfortunate realization that I was not created to cut corners like other people do. Obviously, I've tried again and again and it never works. So I guess I will try to do something inspirational and life-changing. My biggest goal right now is to inspire people. Even someone (singular) whether it's with my story or just inspire someone to see his or her potential. I think that's the greatest gift an individual can give to the world. I don't have any specifics yet on that goal, but my motivator word, for now, is "inspire."

I love you and Luth so much and thank God every day for you(s).

Ok bye.

xoxo,
Lou

p.s have a nice vacation

The above letter was written during Sarah's second rehab placement. She was 19, had just been arrested and charged with drug possession and was assigned to the City of Buffalo Drug Court. Her introspection is simultaneously earnest, sweet and pain-filled. "Luth," as Sarah called him, is my husband, Luther Robinson. Sarah never referred to him as her stepfather. He was more than that to her. They mutually settled on "guardian" which reflected his deep love and protection for Sarah.

W hat she wrote was true. I had rebelliously married a man who had great potential and a not-so-great cocaine addiction. He expressed a desire to know Christ and I truly thought he could just stop using if he really wanted to. In my mind, love would win out, he would stop using drugs and life would be great. I was so very wrong.

My faith was also immature. I had no real-life experience to correctly apply the Scriptures to difficult situations. I thought Philippians 4:13, "I can do all things through Christ who strengthens me," meant that Jesus would strengthen me to convince my husband to become sober. Now, with hard-earned wisdom and hindsight, I know it to mean submitting to God's plan for my life. By the grace of God and not my nagging he did eventually become sober.

Our years together were chaotic. We were always recovering from something: my husband's addiction or my lack of understanding the depth of it. And yet, despite the misery in our marriage, I wanted a child. As things slightly improved, I became pregnant; I miscarried at 12 weeks. We were so broken by this loss. We both knew deep down our marriage wouldn't survive but the urge to have a child persisted. I naively prayed, "Lord please give me a baby…even if I have to raise the child alone."

Things never to say to an omniscient God…

The Lord heard my cry. Sarah's father (along with serious ovulation monitoring and feminine coercion) blessed me with Sarah Louise, 7 lbs., 4 oz., of joy at 4:07 AM on August 28, 1994. She was a beautiful, round-headed screamer. We called her "Baby Round Head." She was perfect. Three months later my husband left.

"…even if I have to raise her alone."

Sarah and I moved to a small apartment and for the next six years had unending adventures—simple, free and fun. We lived frugally (an understatement), but the Lord always provided. Sarah sang continuously, was completely in love with Davy Jones for reasons unknown and was incredibly creative. She was close with her grandparents, aunts, uncles and cousins. We were a statistically "broken family," but we were full of joy and had Christ at the center of our lives.

Sarah's father did the best he could with the skills he had. We are on good terms today, and I will always be grateful for the Lord's using him to grant me a child. In 2004, when Sarah was 10 years old, I married Dr. Luther K. Robinson, a good man who was (and is!) fun, gentle, loving and a strong believer. Luther was kind to Sarah and he loved her deeply. The three of us had a beautiful, simple, loving family filled with travels and the excitements and boredoms of daily life (Luther's three children were grown and living out of town).

As our story picks up in these pages, you will see that Sarah's journal entries represent the conflicts of believers who struggle with addiction. My written commentary attempts to explain the response of a believing loved one. As those who follow Christ, we are often reluctant to see the inner torment of others because pink and glittery is so much easier than ministering to deep, often painful needs. We toss scripture verses like confetti and expect them to penetrate the vulnerable hearts of those who are addicted, while never sticking around to help them live these scriptures out.

What I've learned from Sarah is that I couldn't rescue her from her addiction no matter how hard my mama's heart willed. I couldn't lift her guilt or shame. I couldn't make her whole or give her dignity. But Jesus could and He did. He redeemed Sarah from the pit over and over again. He was truly a well deeper than her thirst. As He was yesterday for Sarah, He is today for you and me.

Scriptures for Consideration

Psalm 42:7 (NIV) *"Deep calls to deep at the roar of Your waterfalls; all Your waves and Your breakers have swept over me."*

Exodus 14:14 (NIV) *"The Lord will fight for you; you need only be still."* (Sarah's choice)

Matthew 25:40 (NIV) *"The King will reply, 'Truly I will tell you, whatever you did for one of the least of these brothers and sisters of mine, you did for me."*

Music to Inspire

"I'm a Believer," The Monkees, (Sarah's choice)
"Through the Fire," Chaka Khan
"Raise a Hallelujah (live)," Jonathan and Melissa Heller
"Even If," Mercy Me
"You Say," Lauren Daigle

Finding Faith, Failing—Repeat

"But put on the Lord Jesus Christ, and make no
provision for the flesh to fulfill its lusts."
Romans 13:14 (NKJV)

December 12, 2017

Lord, I have been a mocker. I have been hiding behind my
bible without ever reading it. By going to bible study, etc., high
I am mocking Christ. That is literally the last thing I'd ever
want to be doing. But, I'll bet Satan is laughing hysterically
at me, and God because he has made me make fun of God
without me even realizing it.

God, I beg for your forgiveness right now. Holy Spirit-I
beg you to enter my heart and help me fight through this sick-
ness and mental obsession. I am done with being bound and
chained by the world. By addiction and chasing heroin daily
no matter what. Jesus has not been on the throne of my heart
recently—if ever. And I so desperately want Him there. I so

desperately want to be used by you Father. I want to know you, Jesus. I want to call you Savior and friend. Lord, I need your help and saving grace. I REFUSE to deny your name anymore. Have mercy on my black heart Father. Holy is your name.

May 2, 2018

Lord God, Jehovah Rapha, the Great Healer, merciful Savior, I am begging and pleading for deliverance from this way of life. I can't stand being so far apart from you Father. I am spiritually starving and withering. My Spirit wants so badly to chase after you but my feet run the opposite way every time I get a chance. Guide my steps Father, even the babiest, tiniest steps Lord.

Praise Your Name,
Amen

May 2, 2019

*...Anyway, I get so unsatisfied, so I get a lil' bit of rock, like a $20 or so. Smoke it. And it's not enough. So of course I must shoot it! The obsession that comes along with the needle is no ** joke y'all. Fast, straight like a punch to the head...and since I don't know what a crack OD feels like (like a dope one I know what it feels like) I always think if I do too much that I am going to have a heart attack and die. So then I panic and write "goodbye letters." This was going to be one but instead, I would like to write about writing either for me to look back on and take a peek at how insane I was, or in case I actually do die this time.*

...Like lately I have been trying to figure out how through my whole messed up addicted trash bag excuse for

a life, my faith in God has never been questioned. The past few days I've been thinking about that a lot. I've gotten very angry with Him of course-but looking back it's more lack of understanding than actual malice. But it's just so foreign to me that so many people struggle with the concept of God and His Son. Like to me it just is...ha-ha... He said, "I Am." Lol ok, HE JUST IS in my mind and my parents have definitely made that faith ever more concrete by seeing them be literal vessels for Him.

And my anger basically comes from-Why can't that be me? I love you too Jesus, and I don't understand why I don't let you take a hold of me fully. It is angering for the fact that it sure isn't for the lack of want to surrender to Him and it surely isn't for wanting to be a complete vessel for Him because that is literally what I want most, more than like a career or beauty or material stuff or status...but my stupid f-ing addiction ruins our connection every single time I have genuinely tried. Consciously, I surely don't want to be destroying my body and cutting off my connection with the One who adores me completely.

Again now back to my frantically scrawled goodbye letter things, if I were to die then, with my heart beating irregularly and dangerously, shaking, panicking; another main thing that I'm feeling about dying then and there is being disappointed. Disappointed because I don't want to die an addict's death. Disappointed because I did not do anything to further God's kingdom.

Sarah wrote the struggles we witnessed daily: repeatedly believing she was having a heart attack and negotiating a trip to the emergency room. Was she attention seeking? Do we wait and see what happens? Divinely granted self-control led us through many of these desperate moments. We worked hard not to overreact every time Sarah said she wanted to die or overdosed. We failed often but learned to trust God with both her addiction and her relationship with Him. It was hers. It was personal and we respected that regardless of how heart-wrenching it was.

As it was with Sarah, "Guide my step, Father," spoken from my heart was a gentle (or sometimes NOT so gentle) ask with hands wide open. Jesus, please let your Word stand as truth in my life. Jesus, please stay close to me. Jesus, please guide me.

These humble yet bold requests were a result of family, friends, pastors and mentors who poured God's truth into us throughout our lives. By the time I was in sixth grade I had "confessed with my mouth that Jesus is Lord and believed in my heart that God raised Him from the dead." (Romans 10:9). I believed that in whatever circumstance, He would never leave me or turn His back on me (Hebrews 13:5 personified). This knowledge became invaluable to me as I made mistakes as a teen, a wife and then as a mother. I was rightly taught that God is a good God and He desires good things for His children (Jeremiah 29:11), a truth I clung to as I watched my first marriage fail and my only child sink into addiction.

God's Word also taught that even though my marriage was a failure, I was not. I was loved and He would teach me how to boldly confess my pride and repent. What a beautiful act of mercy the Lord showed me, allowing me to draw near to Him once again. He trained me to keep my eyes fixed on Him and to stand firm on His word when everything seemed overwhelming. He kept my heart humble.

On the day Sarah's father left, I gathered my prayer warriors together. We prayed, "Lord, protect that man as he chooses to walk in his own wisdom. Protect Sarah and me. Please provide for us." Day by day, He met all of our needs. Maybe not in the exact way I asked but as the Lord rightfully determined. God is just that good.

Believing His Word as truth regardless of what the world was telling me kept doubt, anger and bitterness from consuming me. It allowed me to stay present and in the moment and not to be consumed by the "what ifs" of tomorrow. There were days when I could do nothing but cling to those promises.

As Sarah and I lived paycheck to paycheck in our tiny apartment, I began to trust the Lord with more areas of my life, especially finances. During this season of new obedience, our pastor preached a two-minute sermon one Sunday. He read a scripture I can't remember and said something in the kindest voice like, "You either want some of God's blessings or all of His blessings." He then sat down for 15 minutes of the most uncomfortable silence I had ever endured. It wasn't intimidation from the pulpit, but a time of internal reflection and prayer. The Holy Spirit convicted me and from that day on, I tithed a full 10% of my gross pay before even looking at the bills. Oh, how the Lord was faithful! Every month there were ten dollars left over when the account should have been in the deep zero negatives. (I am no longer bound by the 10% principle but am able to give generously from the abundance of my heart. His growth in me never stops.)

Five years later I bought a house with an insufficient down payment in a highly sought-after neighborhood. Only God! The next year, Sarah and I went to Disney World for a week on a budget of $500, flights included! I would have stayed in my little apartment with my leftover ten dollars every month and continued doing only free things but the Holy Spirit put those ideas in my head and pushed me, uncomfortably, to look outside of myself and trust God with blind faith. I didn't do this alone either. The Lord sent me cheerleaders along the way and prayer partners to support my walk. Yes, we continued to live paycheck to paycheck but we also enjoyed God's incredible blessings along the way.

That is the faith with which Sarah was raised. It wasn't a boring Bible study. It was a daily life lesson in which we saw the Lord's faithfulness, His provision and His protection. We witnessed Jesus' grace poured out upon us as we made mistakes in our relationship. We embraced the power of the Holy Spirit and His constant guidance from day to day. Our life wasn't easy, but it was filled with an active faith in a Triune God.

As Sarah grew older and became more independent, we made a "faith agreement"—I wouldn't browbeat her with Jesus and she wouldn't argue about attending church activities. The rule was only that she had to show up with a respectful attitude; I had to trust that God would do the rest. It worked (for the most part). There were times when Sarah felt left out at youth group or thought church was corny, but she still went.

By the grace of God, Sarah always had a special connection with the Lord. Early one morning, at the age of two or three (she spoke in complete sentences at a very early age), Sarah asked me while she was playing with her doll, "Mama, did you see that man last night?"

"No?" I replied, shocked, "Where was he?"

"Right there!" she said, pointing to the little hallway between our bedrooms.

My heart began pounding. We had a neighbor who loved to peek through our windows. I forced myself to calmly respond, "What did the man do?"

"He looked in your room and then he looked at me."

"What did you do?" I asked as I thought about how quickly I could call 911.

"I waved. He was nice and waved back."

Ok, really??? "How did he leave?" I asked.

"Through the wall, MAMA!" she replied in a disgusted voice and returned to play with her dolly.

After a few moments of pondering, I concluded she must have seen an angel. Hebrews 13:2 does speak of entertaining them, right? While I argued with myself about the reality of such an occurrence, Sarah continued to affirm this angelic visit all of her life. This was the first of many deeply spiritual things I would ponder about my Sarah Lou (one of her many nicknames).

When Sarah was four years old, we had finished dinner and out of the blue, she boldly declared that she wanted Jesus in her heart. I asked Sarah to tell me who Jesus was, what He did for her and what it meant to have Jesus in her heart. I don't remember all of her words, but four-year-old Sarah left the room and some adult version of her confessed her faith in Jesus Christ. We prayed and she went back to being four. I had to learn quickly not to be blown away by what the Lord would do in and through my daughter.

Throughout her elementary and teen years, Sarah asked good, solid theological questions regardless of her age. One of her favorite Sunday school classes was an elementary school study of "The Pilgrim's Progress." While the class studied the book all year, Sarah finished the book in a week (as with most of the books she read) and asked an endless amount of profound questions. I spent a lot of time saying, "I don't know, but I'll get back to you." I was so grateful when Luther and I married so he could help me wade these deep waters with Sarah. The two of them developed a great love of discussing the Scriptures together. More divine provision for a mother with a challenging daughter full of important questions.

As she grew, we saw her witness to children and adults in India, St. Vincent and the Grenadines and South Africa with the innocence of youth and the understanding of an adult. On one particular high school mission trip to St. Vincent, our group was praying for children and their parents in the hospital. We approached a woman and the Holy Spirit prompted me to have Sarah pray for her. She shyly but obediently began and then she stopped and asked if she could continue to pray with the mother in private. Sarah then revealed the woman's life story. The woman was shocked. After assuring the woman no confidentiality laws had been broken, the woman prayed and received healing from some very deep wounds. This was my kid. Lord?

Sarah often wondered why the Lord chose her to receive such knowledge. I did too. It often seemed too much for her young years and created estrangement from those who were still enjoying age-appropriate faith. During times like these, I would seek the Lord and beg Him to make Sarah fit in. He encouraged me through prayer and scripture to trust Him. Sometimes He would do it gently and sometimes rather Job-esquely, "Where were YOU when I laid the foundations of the earth?" (Job 38:4). Ouch.

As for Sarah, this feeling of spiritually not quite fitting in intensified insecurities about her appearance and other "normal" teen issues. Like most kids, she went to youth group grumpy and dragged her feet going to church. Like most moms, I just had to trust that the Lord would open her heart.

One particularly sassy Sunday, when Sarah was about 13, she insisted on wearing a sheer, cream-colored dress to church—the kind that comes with a slightly less sheer slip. Despite our telling her that one could see through it, Sarah rolled her eyes and insisted on wearing the dress. The clock was ticking and tensions were running high. I yelled. Luther yelled. Sarah yelled. Luther and I stepped back and decided we had two choices: make her change and everyone goes to church angry or let her wear the dress and suffer any embarrassment that might come her way. We gave Sarah one last opportunity to change. She refused and off to church we went. Luther and I avoided all eye contact. My mom asked me quietly during service if I had seen what Sarah was wearing. "Yep." Thank goodness I have praying parents!

Once home, without another word spoken, Sarah quietly changed and slipped the offending dress in the donation bag. Years later she would ask us in her self-deprecating way, "WHYYYYYY would you EVER let me wear THAT dress to church???" It became a great source of humor for the three of us.

I tell you these stories so that you can see we had a typical child who did normal, naughty things, but still loved the Lord. So this raises the question: if Sarah loved the Lord so much, how did she end up addicted?

I am not sure I can separate those two. Much like King David, Sarah made choices that were terrible, ugly and self-destructive but much like King David, her heart loved the Lord like nobody I knew. She reminded us of Paul in Romans 7:19, when he spoke about the desire to do right but not having the ability to do so. Her flesh and mind were at war. Oh, but her heart desired His glory; a perfect storm of sorts. This was no secret to any of us or to Sarah, who often articulated this dualism in her journal entries.

To outsiders, Sarah's struggles seemed so simple—just stop being self-destructive! Surrender! But Jesus knew Sarah's battle and stayed by her side until she could no longer fight on her own. Perhaps she struggled like most of us with Galatians 3:3, where our early faith that is led by the Holy Spirit gets derailed by our fleshly attempts to please the Lord. Did she have a confused form of surrender? I don't know. But I do know that in her weakness His grace was sufficient. No abandonment or punishment. Her self-made consequences were punishment enough. God's love for Sarah was deep and everlasting. Their relationship was sealed the day she invited Him into her heart. I will never know why the Lord didn't heal Sarah on earth. I just know that He promised to heal her and He did.

Scriptures for Consideration

Isaiah 25:4-5 (NLV) *"You have been a strong place for those who could not help themselves and for those in need because of much trouble. You have been a safe place from the storm and a shadow from the heat. For the breath of the one who shows no pity is like a storm against a wall. Like a heat in a dry place, You quiet the noise of the strangers. Like heat by the shadow of a cloud, the song of the one who shows no pity is made quiet."*

2 Corinthians 12:9 (NIV) *"But he said to me, 'My grace is sufficient for you, for my power is made perfect in weakness.' Therefore I will boast all the more gladly of my weaknesses, so that the power of Christ may rest upon me."*

Matthew 6:33 (KJV) *"But seek ye first the kingdom of God and His righteousness; and all these things may be added unto you."*

Romans 10:8-9 (ESV) *"…The word is near you, in your mouth and in your heart (that is the word of faith that we proclaim); because, if you confess with your mouth that Jesus is Lord and believe in your heart that God raised him from the dead, you will be saved."*

John 3:16-17 (NKJV) *"For God so loved the world that He gave His only begotten Son that whoever believes in Him shall not perish but have eternal life. For God did not send his Son into the world to condemn the world, but in order that the world might be saved through Him."*

Romans 13:14 (NKJV) *"But put on the Lord Jesus Christ, and make no provision for the flesh to fulfill its lusts." (Sarah's choice)*

Music to Inspire

"Reckless Love," Cory Asbury (Sarah's choice)
"Let it Be," The Beatles
"Salvation is Here," Hillsong United
"Oh, How I love Jesus," Reba McEntire

Chapter 3

Transforming Faith

"The night is far spent, and the day is at hand.
Therefore let us cast off the works of darkness
and let us put on the armor of light."
Romans 13:12 (KJV)

Undated

Sweet Jesus,

Father, you are enough and always have been. It is so hard sometimes Lord to see and feel like you are all I need to be validated, so forgive me, Father. I seek all these other things to make me feel whole and worthy and the answer will always be You.

Thank you, Lord for what you did on the cross for a sinner like me. Thank you for loving me enough to lay your life down so I could be free from the wage of sin. Praise you Lord for defeating Satan on Calvary. Sometimes I feel like he has such power over the world that it seems overwhelming. But thank you for your still small voice reminding me that he has no power over me, so long as I delight in You.

Thank you for rescuing me from the bondage of sin and the shame of addiction Lord. Thank you for opening my eyes to what a precious gift life is and how You have given me so much grace. Father, I have so much to be thankful for it is unreal. Although it is frustrating to lack material things, You have provided me with the things that actually matter in the grand scheme of things. You are so powerful God that I would be foolish to think You would not provide me with the material things that I need when You see fit.

Thank you for opening my mind and my heart.

Your Child,
Sarah

February 22, 2018

I believe today I was made something close to whole so I'm not sure why I still have a strong urge to use if I'm "whole." I'm not doubting God's power at all-but I feel that there is still a small hole that I'm not sure what fragment goes there. I hope I find out/it is revealed.

Without these letters, it would be easy to lose sight of who Sarah really was; the tender-hearted little girl who loved God and loved people. She never said many warm and fuzzy things to anyone but would encourage people through humor and a good sing-a-long. Anyone who knew Sarah can associate a memory of her with a song, whether it was made-up or car karaoke. When I would hear her singing loudly in her bedroom, I knew there was someone on the other end of the phone singing too, followed by laughter and ending inevitably in tears.

Sarah's quirky love language that reached my very soul is one of the things about her I miss the most.

As Sarah sought to offer a healing salve and desperately prayed one of her own, I learned that we don't get to choose on which side of heaven our healing comes. This concept was pretty foreign to me for a long time. My understanding grew with books like "50 Days of Heaven" by Randy Alcorn, which helped me embrace an eternal perspective. But there was another part of me that questioned, "Shouldn't I expect to see my fervent prayers answered? Shouldn't Sarah be able to live in freedom here on earth?" It all seemed so hopeless until I realized that I was crying out to an eternal God who always has an eternal, perfect perspective on all things. If I came to Him with a finite prayer request that I believed was boxed in by space and time, then I did not fully surrender my request to the Lord. His perspective is both momentary and continuous. Mind blowing, right?

Matthew 18:18 reads, "what is bound on earth is also bound in heaven." So when I prayed that Sarah would no longer be bound by addiction, my request was "bound on earth." If my prayer was in accordance with God's will, it was then "bound in heaven." But, the fulfillment of this prayer, whether on earth or in heaven, could only be experienced with a surrendered and repentant heart on Sarah's behalf. Only God knew when and where my prayer would be fulfilled.

I learned to hang in that submissive balance, understanding that absolutely nothing will happen without His permission. In His space and time. For Sarah that meant that sometimes she was completely broken and deeply repentant, seeking forgiveness and trying to make small, positive changes that would glorify God. In that, I could see the evidence of answered prayers. At other times, when her depression and addiction worsened, I would have to walk by faith, still praying but understanding the control was God's, not mine.

I had to completely surrender my pleas, trusting that He knew the perfect moment to fulfill my requests and hers. My surrender ranged from sweet to reluctant. There were nights Sarah was missing and I would turn her over to the Lord and sleep peacefully. Other nights, I would pace the floor, fending off anxiety, "telling" the Lord over and over that Sarah was His and not mine. I would concede permission to do whatever He needed to do with her because He had the perfect plan and I did not. These were grueling exercises in obedience. Either way, my submission brought honor to the Lord and He was glorified by my feeble attempts at giving up the control I thought I had.

Only the Father knows what was in Sarah's heart and mind as she breathed her last breath. And that is where I rest in faith knowing that His timing was perfect and her surrender complete. I just know that Sarah is free today. Her eternal life is free from the bondage of depression and addiction. Twenty-five years is just a blip on the radar of eternity and despite the pain of missing my girl daily, I can still call that victory.

For our part, Sarah's long spiritual battle made us that much more aware of sin's devastating nature. Sin always separates, distorts and destroys our healthy choices. Satan takes those poor choices and anchors them in guilt and shame to try and separate us from the Lord (Ephesians 6:16). He tried with every minion, demon, and form of oppression to do this with Sarah. Yet, despite what it looked like on the outside, Sarah's faith and knowledge of Christ deepened in inexplicable ways. Whenever we thought she was too far gone, Sarah would surprise us with insight from her Bible readings or a podcast discussion that would lead us into mutually edifying conversations. Pastor Paul Shepard of "Destined for Victory" was one of her favorite podcast hosts. She loved his practical application of scripture and his good humor, the combination of which appealed to her quirky nature.

During the course of Sarah's life on earth, the Lord taught me that faith and tribulation are intimate friends. By faith through tribulations, He taught me how to fight—how to lean on Him and to stand firm on His Word.

One day in the early part of Sarah's drug use, as I was in my prayer closet praising, crying and shouting to the Lord (this closet also doubled as my real closet and happened to be very close to my neighbor's driveway), I heard a loud banging at my door. Bang, bang, bang. Darn. Maybe if I stay quiet, whoever it is will go away? Bang, bang, bang. Ugh. I pulled myself together and answered the door to find my next-door neighbor looking very concerned.

"Is everything alright?" he asked.

"Yes, of course," I said, with all the confidence I could muster.

"Are you sure you're okay?" he asked as he looked over my shoulder to see if anyone was with me.

"Yep, just fine." Awkward pause. "Why do you ask?"

"Well, I heard a lot of yelling going on and I just wanted to make sure you were okay."

"Oh," I said sheepishly. "I was just having a chat with the Lord."

"Okay...('weirdo,' I'm sure he was saying in his head). Call me if you need me."

Outside, later that day, he asked me if I really talked to the Lord like that. I had the opportunity to share how I trusted the Lord to hear my prayers through my yelling/crying/stamping and that, oh yes, supplicating is really messy. I told him how the Lord wants us to draw near to Him with complete and unabashed transparency and in return, He will hear our cries, soothe our hearts and give us the strength to continue (Psalm 86:1-17). While he still looked at me a bit sideways, my neighbor, with his mustard seed faith, grew to become one of Sarah's greatest prayer intercessors.

As Sarah's depression deepened and her addiction escalated, I needed to depend more and more on the Lord. I HAD to pray constantly. I HAD to read the Bible. I HAD to spend time with family and friends who would not ask a million probing questions but agree with me in prayer. Sarah's life and my sanity depended on it.

As the intensity of our situation increased, the Lord dared me to be creative in my relationship with Him and with Sarah. I learned to be bold in my prayer requests. I learned to listen for that still small voice of the Holy Spirit and to be obedient. I let Sarah go even when my flesh wanted to hold her back. I laid my hands on her and prayed for protection, healing, and deliverance and she allowed it every time. If you have teenagers or young adults in your life, you will understand how miraculous this was.

One of the creative ways the Holy Spirit inspired me was to use Sarah's favorite childhood doll affectionately named "Stinky." Sarah had received Stinky on her first birthday and refused to change the poor doll's name once she had given it. Stinky slept with her every night until she was about 10 years old. When Sarah was 19, she refused to come home from wherever she was. I knew she was in danger. I begged the Lord to give me some comfort; I needed to hold my baby. As I was praying, the idea "popped" into my head to get Stinky out of storage. I dug her out of a box, wiped the dust off and began praying over this doll as if she were Sarah. I anointed Stinky with oil, laid my hand on the doll's heart and prayed for Sarah. I touched her head and prayed for wisdom.

Sarah didn't come home that night and while my actions seemed a bit crazy, the Lord gave me a peace that passes all understanding through that funny little doll. For the next six years, Stinky would sit on my nightstand, waiting to be called into service. The Holy Spirit used that doll to ease my heart in a tangible, effective way. Today, Stinky hangs out in the guest room, occasionally offering me a bit of my girl for just a while longer.

You may be wondering why I continued to fervently pray to God when no evidence of Sarah's deliverance was seen. I will tell you that despite every arrest, overdose, homeless period, program, court obligation and friends' funerals, the Lord blessed Sarah and me with an unbreakable bond. Our relationship was a gift from God and we worked hard to maintain it. He knew we needed a good, solid, fun, sad, beautiful relationship. A relationship similar to what the Lord desires with each of us. Sarah and I loved hard and fought hard. Every terrifying, heart-wrenching effort was worth it. It wasn't what I prayed for but He heard my cries and He answered me (Psalm 120:1) with an answer only He could foresee.

Luther and I learned to trust the Holy Spirit completely. Scripture says that the "Father would send us another Helper" (John 14:16a). We desperately needed His help!

On several occasions, the Holy Spirit woke us up in the middle of the night with persistent urges to get out of bed. We just wanted to sleep. When we finally got up, the Spirit directed us to wherever we needed to go. Many times it was downstairs to the computer where Sarah had left her messenger app open which would tell us exactly where she was. Thank you, Holy Spirit.

As Sarah's addiction worsened, so did the dangers. One night we were getting ready for bed and I felt the urging of the Holy Spirit to get in the car. I grabbed my husband and told him we needed to drive somewhere. We dashed into the car and Luther assumed I knew where we were going. Nope. I was silently praying, "Now what, Holy Spirit?"

"Just tell him to drive." So I did.

"Drive where?" Luther asked.

"I don't know. Just keep driving till I tell you to turn."

My husband is a patient man, but this had him annoyed. It was late and it was cold. "Where are we going?" he asked again in a firm, staccato voice. "Where. Are. We. Going?"

"You just have to trust me. I'll tell you when the Holy Spirit tells me." Miraculously, and because he is a man of faith, Luther just started driving. On and on it went. I'd hear the Holy Spirit like a voice in my head say, "Drive to the city. Take this route. Turn here. Go faster. Now slower. Stop here," until we saw her running down a street that we'd never been on before. When Sarah got in the car, she was a sobbing mess, amazed that we found her.

It only took that one time for Luther to be a willing and faithful participant in the future. Sometimes we would arrive at a trap house (drug house) or other unsafe location. Should we call the police? Go in? Both? Neither? We would pray and wait. Sometimes, the Holy Spirit just wanted us to know where she was and we would return home. Sometimes legal interventions were needed and sometimes I knew it was safe enough for me to go in while Luther stayed close by. Sarah did not always appreciate our interventions, but we didn't care. Our obedience was to Christ and His guidance to find her served as a testimony of His love for her.

As her disease progressed and her situations grew dire, Sarah would tell us that she would just wait for us to show up. Just like Luther and I were leaning on the Holy Spirit, she was too. We learned the importance of spiritual obedience. If we weren't supposed to go and we went anyway, the situation invariably turned into a debacle. We gradually learned that submission was always better than sacrifice (I Samuel 15:22 NLT).

The times when the Lord would tell us to wait were the most difficult. "But Lord?!" "No, my child, wait." "But, but, but, but????" "Wait." He needed us to trust Him in new ways. He wanted to broaden our understanding of who He was and is to us. In those times, I would seek out and read scriptures that would encourage me as I waited. The faith of Rahab, the strength of Joshua and the tearful obedience of Jeremiah would let me know that I was not alone. I praise God for the growth that those precarious but obedient times gave us in our faith. I serve a good God who was willing to teach me in all situations. I just had to listen.

I would find myself lost in a scripture from which the Lord wouldn't release me. Day after day of reading the same verses over and over. What was I missing? What did You want me to see? A week would go by. Then two. A month later, LET ME OUT OF HERE!

During one prolonged instance, I sat in Hebrews chapters 9, 10, and 11 for what seemed like an eternity. I read over and over of Christ's perfect sacrifice, the confidence of our faith and examples of faith applied. I would pray, worship and then ask the Lord to lead me (hopefully out of this book!). But nope, there I sat. Eventually, when I stopped being disgusted that I was STILL required to be in the same chapters, the Lord began to speak to my heart. The sacrifice of Jesus' life and His resurrection are imperative to the Christian faith. Without Christ's life, death and resurrection, my faith, future and works are empty. This process became an intimate time of worship and adoration for me. I knew that I might never see Sarah free, but there was more to her life than her freedom from drugs. He taught me to cherish her love for Him over anything else.

Hebrews Chapter 11 is known as the faith chapter. The spiritual legends live there (Noah, Abraham, Isaac, Sarah and others). The Lord would lead me to that chapter and say, "See how weak so and so was, but look what I did? Now look at so and so, complete knucklehead, but did you see how I used him? Isn't that great, Sandi?" God's faithfulness to ordinary people in extraordinary ways was revealed, pushing and encouraging me to keep going. I wish I could say it was easy and that I always understood what the Lord was doing. I didn't. I fought with the Lord. Shook my fists at Him. Oh, but He was so patient. He would wait until my flesh was tired and my pride was ready to be laid aside. Then He would scoop me up and wrap His invisible blanket around me to comfort me once again.

A little over a year before Sarah died, Luther and I were working outside. He was pulling weeds and I was watering the flowers. It was not a time of crisis and Sarah was clean. Out of the blue, I heard a very audible man's voice say, "I'm going to take her." I turned around to look but nobody was in our yard. It wasn't a scary voice but one of gentle authority. The tears instantly started flowing from my eyes and I knew the Lord was preparing me for Sarah's death.

I didn't say anything to Luther but quickly dropped the hose and went inside and sobbed. It really made no sense to my practical mind. Lord, was that really you? Sarah seems fine. Maybe You meant you were going to replace the old Sarah with the new healed one? No answer. This began a two-week surreal grieving period. I mentally and emotionally battled with the reality of the Lord's statement and my grief. Poor Luther could only watch and trust that God was doing something deep within me.

A couple of days into this bizarre, other-worldly experience I called a dear friend for input. Was I going mad? Did I really hear His voice? She gently listened and prayed with me. She knew grief well. Her addicted family member had been murdered and her own healing had taken her through many years of trusting God with her pain and sorrow. Following our conversation, she brought me over the devotional, "50 Days of Heaven: Reflections That Bring Eternity to Light" by Randy Alcorn. It was the single most encouraging book on grief and the gift of heaven I have read. I treasured those pages during months of long, slow readings. No, I would not know when Sarah would be healed or taken from this earth, but I knew Jehovah Rapha, our healer, would be the one to do it. I never gave up hope that I would see her healed on earth but also prayed that His will would be done.

I tucked these lessons and experiences away and continued on with the business of living without the constant fear of what the Lord was going to do.

Eventually, I forgot about the garden encounter. The Lord brought it gently back to my memory about a week after Sarah's death while we were in Florida making her funeral arrangements. This time, I was so grateful. I wasn't overwhelmed or consumed with grief. I now had a scriptural and eternal perspective that included a loving God, a perfect plan and my daughter.

It was all so miraculous, especially at a time when safety, peace and travel were a challenge due to the COVID-19 pandemic. My husband and I even had a few wonderful, cherished and humorous moments amidst all the sadness. It was a very precious gift from the Father, joy in the midst of sorrow (2 Corinthians 6:10).

People often comment on how strong we seem. Faith and boldness often look like we are the strong ones. It is the Lord's strength and wisdom that are remarkable. The Lord is the one who has the faith that can move mountains. Therefore, my faith has to look like blind trust, feet firmly planted on His Word, taking baby steps on only the path He has lit. And that is just what we did for days that turned to years.

I wish Sarah could have read Jackie Hill-Perry's latest book, "Holier than Thou." Man, she would have received Jackie's deep-seated truth. It's not about the name or shame of the sin, it's about God's holiness. "Holier Than Thou" continues to help me make sense of Sarah's struggles and my own. Read it. You will not be disappointed.

Sarah and I each traveled a faith journey of confession, repentance, growth and blind faith. In her journal entries, you can experience Sarah's battle between her mind and the Truth. You see her disappointment of not being able to further the kingdom of God. Yet her living testimony proves otherwise. Since her death, many people have contacted me about Sarah's positive influence on their own walk with Christ. There is little I could have added to Sarah's writings and her heart's desire to serve the Lord. I pray that as you read her entries you begin to understand the struggle of addiction and the journey of faith that are never mutually exclusive.

Scriptures for Consideration

I Corinthians 13:12 (KJV) *"For now we see in a mirror, darkly, but then face-to-face: now I know in part; but then shall I know fully even as also I was fully known."*

Jeremiah 31:3 (NIV) *"The Lord appeared to us in the past, saying: 'I have loved you with an everlasting love; I have drawn you with unfailing kindness.'"*

Romans 13:12 (KJV) *"The night is far spent, and the day is at hand. Therefore let us cast off the works of darkness and let us put on the armor of light."* (Sarah's choice)

Proverb 22:6 (KJV) *"Train up a child in the way he should go, and when he is old he will not depart from it."*

Music to Inspire

"Can't Give Up Now," Mary Mary
"You Reign," William Murphy
"Something in the Water," Carrie Underwood
"Holy Spirit Rain Down," Hillsong

Chapter 4

Depression

"For He satisfies the longing soul,
and fills the hungry soul with goodness."
Psalm 107:9 (ESV)

I n one journal entry, Sarah described her depression; *"throughout my childhood and early adulthood, I've been plagued with an ever-present sadness. I was never absolutely sure where this heaviness came from, as I had never been exposed to any trauma."*

Her definition was rather textbook. The Mayo Clinic website states that, "depression is a mood disorder that causes a persistent feeling of sadness and loss of interest. Also called major depressive disorder or clinical depression, it affects how you feel, think and behave and can lead to a variety of emotional and physical problems. You may have trouble doing normal day-to-day activities, and sometimes you may feel as if life isn't worth living." (Mayo Clinic-syc 20356007, February 3, 2018)

May 30, 2011

My friend Timmi was saying the other day how everyone has more bad or good traits. I asked her what she thinks I have, and she just said, "sad traits." Maybe that's what I am...a sad human being who doesn't know what she wants out of life. I've been pretty f***ing miserable. Not to mention I'm getting fat from not doing drugs and not going to the gym. All I do is sleep and exist. Yep, that's what I'm doing...existing. Do you ever question why you're here and what you're here for? I want to make a difference in people's lives and not just take up space. That's the type of person I want to be.

February 24, 2019

Today has been incredibly strange. I am having trouble remembering things. Like short term...and I can't stand the odd way I'm acting that causes them to keep looking at me a certain way. Again another day wasted in the most unproductive way possible. The winds are so loud and strong. When I feel like this loud strong noises are almost unbearable and harsh. I feel so void. I'm so sad that I missed church again. I could've went and at least sat in the back yet I remain a coward and lie in the bed for the purpose of going back to sleep, but never getting that far. It's just another lame excuse to not have my cup filled.

My cup is completely empty currently and I can't keep this up. I'm so overweight; greasy, barely shower, barely brush my teeth. I have slept an estimated 4-5 hours the past 3 nights! My mrsa infection is disgusting looking; I really don't want to be around people because of how nasty it is BUT I CRAVE others so much. I crave connection with a friend...I think I have zero serotonin/dopamine receptors in my brain at this point. I literally feel no hope-like I cannot think of one thing right now that I can say brings me joy. "Why don't *you do a gratitude list…Appreciate all the things that you have in your life that drugs haven't taken yet." F*** YOUR GRATITUDE LISTS!*

I can say yes I am appreciative of the things in my life that are categorized as what humanity has deemed, "good." But as a feeling I feel no spark towards others. Well good thing it just came to me. GRATITUDE IS AN ACTION WORD! Duh! Totally forgot. I am doing zero action. In fact if there were negative action, I'd be doing that. I'm not proud of that. It's cynical and a little sarcastically humorous, but I absolutely loathe being like this. Who wants to be a shell just breezing by until you die? I really don't.

Undated 2020

I just wanted the pain to stop. Everything I did, I did to make the pain go away but it only got emptier and darker and more scary.

Sarah began exhibiting symptoms of depression in her early elementary school years. She was a classic "old soul" and always had a dry wit, but there were subtle signs that she was struggling in a way I couldn't define. Was she depressed? I simply thought people just didn't understand her. At home she was a creative fun child who loved playing the piano and Barbies, completely age-appropriate activities.

In early elementary Sarah received a referral to the school psychiatrist without my permission. When I questioned the behaviors that would warrant such a referral, I was told, "Sarah doesn't laugh at jokes like the other kids." There were no other behaviors of concern, just Sarah's response to a teacher's humor. Sarah completed all her work, was respectful and not disruptive. "A pleasure to have in class." Hmmm…

When questioned, Sarah said, "Mom, my teacher thinks there's something wrong with me 'cause I don't laugh at her jokes."

"Are they funny?"

"NO!"

"What are the other children doing?"

"Laughing."

"Can you tell me one of her jokes?" She did. I didn't laugh either.

Sarah and I discussed the situation and devised appropriate solutions. The teacher never mentioned a referral for Sarah again and I assumed there were no further concerns. In my heart I knew Sarah was different, but I really didn't think she was depressed. If anything, I would have said she was shy and discerning.

Yet as shy as she was, Sarah could deliver a wicked one-liner that would leave peers confused and adults at first speechless, then laughing. It began as early as age two when, upon being asked the names of her two Sunday School teachers countless times by adults attempting to make toddler conversation, she sweetly responded, "Cain and Abel." Oh, the SHOCK! At least she was paying attention, right? This was my life, smiling politely and making quick escapes while laughing on the inside.

Sometimes Sarah's humor was more of a social experiment to see how people would react. For several years she told her friends that she had a brother who was in a wheelchair and lived in our basement (insert eye roll). After several awkward parental inquiries, I had to have a little chat with my daughter. Sarah was both appalled and amused that people actually took her seriously. It was the beginning of a creative license that tended to make her a bit of a misfit.

By the sixth grade, Sarah began to socially withdraw. She preferred a book to the struggle of social interactions. She read "A Tale of Two Cities," at age nine for fun (when I was reading the Sunday comics).

With Sarah as a willing participant, we tried a host of activities to increase her socialization. Anything with music gave her the greatest measure of comfort: youth choir, musicals, piano, clarinet and voice lessons. Yet all activities were met with limited reward. She even tried softball, volleyball and track. Again, little reward. Nothing quite fit and we told ourselves that Sarah was uniquely herself.

To alleviate any lingering concerns, Sarah saw several counselors and psychologists. We were encouraged when each professional told us "lots of loners grow up to be normal people." Upon their suggestions or some version of the same, we tried to limit Sarah's alone time and insisted that she interact with friends. This was very strenuous for her. She would frequently come home early from social interactions happy, yet completely depleted. A nap always followed even the most enjoyable outings.

When Sarah was brave enough to enter anything competitive, she always came in just behind the victor. "It's not important to be first," we would encourage. "Your instructors are looking at the whole person, not just your talent. Try hard to be a team player." And she would try harder. It was excruciating to watch her take these hits while also battling the symptoms of depression we did not yet understand. I cannot imagine how much more painful it was for Sarah.

Luther would pray and I would plead with the Lord asking, "Why is she not being chosen for *anything*?" The Lord answered me one day, probably around the time she was in seventh grade after yet another heartbreaking disappointment. I heard Him say, "Until Sarah puts me first, she will always be second." I was crushed and like Jacob, wrestled with His words. How do I tell her that? Do I even tell her? She's so young! Like Mary, I tucked those words in my heart and waited for the right time to share this revelation.

Around this same time, Sarah read a fiction book about self-abuse and began to relieve her sadness through cutting. I had noticed that she was wearing long sleeves and pants even though the weather had gotten warmer. One day when we were cuddling, I was rubbing her arm and Sarah winced. I rolled up her sleeves and found slashes everywhere. She was sad, angry and embarrassed. My stomach heaved.

I immediately made an appointment with a psychiatrist friend of ours. Sarah began to see him regularly. As a strong believer, he encouraged Sarah to give her sadness, hurt and pain to the Lord. This faithful and faith-filled servant of the Lord taught her how to talk through issues and how to pray. Healing was possible. He knew her issues were spiritual and did his best to lead her through deep inner healing. He also prescribed Sarah antidepressants for short-term use. He understood depression and knew that healing would take time. After much trial and error, he found a medication that allowed her to think clearly and which alleviated some of her severe symptoms. His practical and spiritual expertise was a gift to us for many years.

As the healing process continued, Sarah grew bolder and tried more social activities and auditions with the same results—second or not chosen at all. In high school, she vocally mastered a 12-page opera piece IN ITALIAN for competition. It was absolutely beautiful. Sarah was so excited to compete. As she waited for her day and time to sing, the music teacher informed her that he "forgot" to submit her application (the only student out of hundreds....). It seemed absolutely unbelievable. Sarah missed the competition and was beyond devastated. We later learned she was collateral damage of a long-held resentment by the music teacher towards the vocal coach.

At this point, I chose to tell Sarah what I believed the Lord had shown me. When I did, there was a knowing look in her eyes that quickly turned to anger. "Why would the same God who says he loves me always make me last?" She felt betrayed by the One she loved. She cried and we talked about it. At the heart level, Sarah was mostly angry that she was called to a deep faith at such a young age. She felt this would make her even more of an outcast. Sarah understood what the Lord was saying to her and yet she hated it.

As Sarah grew, there were times when she would sing for her voice coach, at church or in her room and it was outstanding, the beauty ethereal. I would listen in amazement outside her bedroom door or in the back of the church. She was truly gifted. Sarah would quietly confess to me that these were her "God first" moments. Years later, when the music had long stopped, Sarah wished she had continued to trust the Lord instead of letting hurt and pride get in the way. She deeply missed the way God spoke to her through music performance.

Despite disappointment and depression diagnosis, life was not all bad. We still traveled, laughed, played games, cuddled and genuinely enjoyed each other's company. None of us, including Sarah, realized the depth of her despair until she was hospitalized at the start of her freshman year with a bout of infectious mononucleosis and blood clots in her jugular vein due to a previously unknown genetic clotting disorder. It nearly killed her. She missed months of school. And as happens with teens, when she returned to school, her friends had established new friend groups and she was left to begin again.

Sarah's depression worsened and she moved closer and closer to the kids that would accept her—older, edgier and mutually broken. Sarah began experimenting with cigarettes, marijuana and methamphetamines. The result was increased anxiety, anger and isolation. Once, we returned home to find that her friend had called the police because Sarah was "out of it" and hyperventilating on the front lawn. The scene was bizarre, Sarah lying on the lawn and the police yelling at her. It was our first experience with law enforcement and one of the only times the police offered us no ostensible assistance. Whatever drug she had taken put her in a paranoid state, which caused a full-blown anxiety attack. We asked the police to leave and took Sarah inside to decide our next steps. She calmed down, and as she was telling us what she had taken, a rage overtook her and she smashed her hand through a window. This was enough for us to call an ambulance and have her evaluated. Sadly, these types of incidents would replay horrifically over the next few years.

Sarah graduated from high school early and found herself continually reaping the negative consequences of her pain-motivated choices. Her life was now a downward spiral with few moments of sanity. There was more counseling, more crying and loads of more praying. We would encourage, force her out of bed, yell, hug, hold and beg. We truly did the best we could for Sarah with the tools we had. I have no idea how, in her pervasive sadness, she survived for so long.

*Depression is serious. If you or a family member is suffering from depression or suicidal thoughts, please seek professional help. Call Crisis Services 800.273.8255 or text 839863 24/7 SAMHSA's National Helpline referral and information service: 1.800.662.4357
Check your local listings under Crisis Services or Mental Health Services for support groups and other services.

Scriptures for Consideration

Lamentations 3:22-23 (NIV) *"Because of the Lord's great love we are not consumed, for His compassions never fail. They are new every morning; Great is Your faithfulness."* (Sarah's choice)

Psalm 107:9 (ESV) *"For He satisfies the longing soul, and fills the hungry soul with goodness."* (Sarah's choice)

Deuteronomy 31:8 (NIV) *"The LORD himself goes before you and will be with you; he will never leave you nor forsake you. Do not be afraid; do not be discouraged."*

Psalm 3:3 (NIV) *"But you, LORD, are a shield around me. My glory, the One who lifts my head high."*

I Peter 5:6-7 (NIV) *"Humble yourselves, therefore, under God's mighty hand, that he may lift you up in due time. Cast all your anxiety on him because he cares for you."*

Isaiah 41:10 (NIV) *"Do not fear, for I am with you; do not be dismayed, for I am your God. I will strengthen you and help you; I will uphold you with my righteous right hand."*

Romans 8:28 (NIV) *"And we know that in all things God works for the good of those who love him, who have been called according to his purpose."*

Music to Inspire

"Weep with Me," Rend Collection
"Praise You in This Storm," Casting Crowns
"We Exalt Your Name," Tamela Mann
"Haven't Seen it Yet," Danny Gokey
"You are Not Alone," Michael Jackson
"Burn," Group 1 Crew
"Where Do I Fit In," Justin Bieber

Chapter 5

Addiction

"Teach me to do Your will, for you are my God;
Your Spirit is good.
Lead me in the land of uprightness."
Psalm 143:10 (NKJV)

Late 2017

The first couple of years I dabbled in ecstasy, suboxone various pills, hallucinogens, until finally came the day that I found love at first sight. The first time I tried it I vomited and was rocked. Even so I was instantly in love with heroin. The first time I went to rehab I was taken from my home in the middle of the night by transport agents and shipped all the way to Texas.

Two months after I returned home from Texas, I was introduced to the needle. I had thought I was in love before, but with a spike in my vein I was invincible, I was PERFECT and I was hopelessly in love.

The next couple of years were a jumble of cosmetology school, rehabs and jail.

May 2, 2018

Something was urging me to write tonight...or SOMEONE maybe...hmm...There's so much going on in my head and heart at all times. It's like I don't know where to even start. There is no beginning, middle, end. Events, people, places and whole days even, are basically mashed into one metal box with no oxygen.

Everything I do now revolves around money and dope. It's like I can't even pretend to care about anything else right now-and this particular place is a very scary place to be. A place I desperately want out of. I am constantly praying for the strength to get out of this hole. The thing is the solutions are literally all in front of me. Now, I am praying/begging for the willingness to use said solutions PLEASE GOD! I know that You have been with me through this tortuous walk, please give me the willingness to GIVE UP. To give in and accept the help that is constantly being offered.

I have no idea why it is so hard to admit to people that care about me where I'm really at. I create these exact plans in my head on how I'm going to break down and admit that all of my current problems, are stemming directly from DRUGS, not all this bull**** depression. That is only a small ripple effect from the using. It seems as if my mouth will not let me let the words and confessions pass through my lips! Instead spouts more lies that I can't even keep up with.

This hole in my chest is so deep and dark. His light is going to be the only thing that even stands a chance in the darkness. The drugs are blocking our spirits from connecting, so it's like I'm sabotaging myself to not be healed and be a zombie and a slave. Which brings me to my next question. Why am I so scared (terrified) of being sick [withdrawal]?

It's not just that it sucks, b/c it does. I'm thinking that perhaps the emotional pain attached to the physical withdrawal has a ton to do with it. Put them together and you have physical pain as well as shame and hopelessness so bad that it could almost be physical pain...

May 3, 2018

My tolerance is overwhelmingly high. Guess how many bags I did today? 12. Guess how high I am? I'm not. ...If I'm feeling this completely empty now at 12 bags a day, how much more dope would I have to do in order to cover up the shame, pain and emptiness of the things I'd need to do to keep this up? Enough to sedate a small dinosaur. Most certainly enough to be deadly or at least causing permanent health and bodily damage.

May 23, 2018

I am so wrecked right now. So annoyed at myself. Finally got up the bravery to admit and ask for help....I will finish this later...I am literally...too f-ed up.

May 24, 2018

I am so upset with myself because I'm still using. Did detox for five days. Had someone bring me 2 bags and left the next day. There is something insane inside of me-some little piece of insanity that is literally corrupting the rest of my brain and heart.

May 29, 2018

Gratitude

1. *My family*
2. *That it's not winter*
3. *Sponsor*
4. *Central air*
5. *Clean water*
6. *Faith*
7. *Al & Viv*
8. *A bed*
9. *A beautiful backyard*
10. *Forgiveness*

I almost made it today. I didn't but at least I had genuine second thoughts Man am I tired of being flat lined. I have no real up, no real downs, everything just "is." I want to laugh. I want sorrow. And I want Joy. Right now it is just constant hopelessness. I let myself get so heavy.

Why do I constantly feel the need to escape reality? My life could be really great. I am so blessed and fortunate-Lord I am not understanding. I'm asking and begging you Lord Oh mighty healer!!! Remove the obsession to use drugs to escape reality. Remove the mental compulsion and physical sickness and addiction. Lord be merciful! Give me the motivation and self control to get through the physical ailments. Help me to defend my most deadly enemy-MYSELF.

July 27, 2018

I still feel super empty. Why am I still so stuck in my old ways? It's not like I want to. I need help so bad. I am dying on the inside so bad and I can feel my outside following not long after.
I am terrified...

August 19, 2018

I have been clean for 15 days today. I'm so irritated that I allowed myself to get distracted. I don't think that I ever realized that I did this at almost every point, going into rehab-minus Florida. Even then I wasn't ready.

It's like my mind can never just be ok. It always needs to obsess on one thing or if it's not completely obsessed, it's disinterested. No wonder I went back out every time. Every time I was left with myself, of which I did no actual work on besides removing the drugs.

2019

I'm writing this as a precaution-just because I have a bad sense of foreboding. I don't know why nothing is bad enough for me to stop and save myself. I HATE who I am currently. I legit HATE her-her voice, her laugh, her warped sense of humor and the way she treats others; or doesn't treat them. The real me is buried under layers and layers of concrete SH** made up of compacted lies, manipulation, stolen items, hurt, guilt, shame, rage, jealousy, self pity, ego, terror, homicidal ideations, delusions, false idols etc. So far in my 24 years I have barely made a dent in this lethal pile of sh**. It's always, ok, tomorrow, here I come! The real me is getting freed today! And surprisingly, tomorrow never comes.

Even little Sarah trapped under my sh** dungeon is losing hope. As every year passes, she loses more hope. She is becoming gaunt and frail. Her cheekbones protrude and her eyes pop out. She has very little energy and is waiting to die for good.

Grown Sarah continues on recklessly on the hamster wheel of horror and death. The light is always in view, but the path never gets closer. It stays the same size for copycat Sarah even as she sprints towards it.

Early on, neither Luther, Sarah nor I used the word "addiction" to describe her behavior. It felt like a trap. It actually felt satanic. We all believed that words had power and none of us wanted to speak addiction into existence. A diagnosis of depression had already been a crushing blow. Adding addiction just seemed hopeless. Sarah would tell us it was just a phase and after heroin entered the picture, she would say that she could stop with the right opportunities or environment. We all knew that was impossible but somehow it seemed reasonable to let her try. After repeated attempts at changing her behavior without success we knew addiction was here to stay.

Addiction is defined as a chronic, relapsing brain disease that is characterized by compulsive drug seeking and use, despite harmful consequences. (National Institute on Drug Abuse, revised June 2020)

Addiction is: The state of being compulsively committed to a habit or practice or to something that is physiologically or physically habit-forming, as narcotics, to such an extent that its cessation causes severe trauma. (Dictionary.com 2020)

Addiction is a treatable, chronic medical disease involving complex interactions among brain circuits, genetics, the environment, and an individual's life experiences. People with addiction use substances or engage in behaviors that become compulsive and often continue despite harmful consequences. (American Society of Addiction Medicine, 2019)

And from a pointedly spiritual perspective, addiction is "voluntary slavery" a term coined by Dr. Edward Welch as he began his discussion on the biblical concept of addiction in his work, "Addiction: A Banquet in the Grave" (2001).

Regardless of which definition you choose, addiction is devastating. It is selfish and all-consuming. The act of being compulsively and fatally drawn to destruction so graphically defined Sarah's addiction. Yet true to the conflicting powers of compulsion and choice, she had planted herself firmly in the bondage of addiction when making the decision to use. Sarah desperately sought relief from it and paradoxically in it.

We lived this insane pattern repeatedly with Sarah and her friends. They longed for freedom and at times even walked freely. But inevitably they would succumb to their old desires and choose to find relief with the very same thing that was destroying them. Couldn't they see drugs were ruining their lives? Didn't it bother them to hurt the ones they loved? Why did they keep running into the fire and not away? The simple incomprehensible answer is, they couldn't. They literally couldn't stop themselves. That's the insanity of addiction. It made/makes me very sad and very angry.

I've thought about this a lot and have seen that in our experience addiction began with small, voluntary choices that had real or perceived benefits with limited or no consequences. Like when Sarah began drinking alcohol, smoking pot or taking ecstacy. Her first experiences were fun. She rarely got caught. Using was ironically a much-desired social interaction that had the potential to relieve her depression. Not surprisingly, her repeated use led to more daring choices that eventually resulted in bondage.

In the public view there are good addictions and bad addictions. For people without "bad" addictions, sugar is a good example. If I can eat one cookie without gaining weight or impacting my cholesterol or diabetes, two should be just fine. Soon all the cookies are gone and I'm searching for something else that will fill the sugar void. When Sarah was clean, she would always have a bag of gummy worms stashed in her purse or she would wake up in the middle of the night and eat an entire pan of brownies. The next day she would be sluggish and crabby. It was still addiction but the consequences seemed less harmful. Not a sweets person? Think coffee! Same impact. How many people do you know that literally can't start their day without a cup of coffee and a cigarette! Dare to change that pattern of use abruptly and those negative consequences of headaches and irritability come rolling in.

How about shoplifting, a very common and grossly under-recognized addiction? Sarah was a prolific shoplifter. It began as a way to make money for drugs. And when she discovered how good she was at "boosting," Sarah would steal just for the thrill of it, even if she had money in her pocket. I was appalled when Sarah called me with an attitude from the police station after being detained by mall security. "It was just perfume! The security guard should just mind his own business!" There was no rational response that would change her mind, including jail. I learned to remain silent and allow the consequences to have their own voice, to be her teacher. Yes, I sat with her in court and visited her in jail, but I rarely engaged in nonproductive conversations about her addictions and their consequences unless she asked a specific, forward-moving question. That was both a freeing and frustrating exercise in preserving my sanity and our relationship.

It took me a long time to realize that one doesn't merely overcome addiction with fortitude alone. I spent years in Al-Anon, working the steps, reading AA and NA materials, studying scripture and seeking wise counsel in order to have even a tiny understanding of what addiction looks like in the flesh. Hearing and reading about the paths others have walked was important to me as I understood that we, too, should not be bound by Sarah's addiction lest we develop our own. For my part, I have learned to show grace and sympathy while establishing healthy boundaries.

Addiction also made me re-think the ways in which I love and support others. It made me humble. It made me angry. It gave me a tender heart toward those who are suffering. It challenged me to treat people differently and without judgment. By opening my heart and mind to be teachable, I have gained beautiful, often unlikely friendships and a wisdom that better enables me to understand suffering through the eyes of Christ.

Addiction added a rather forced transparency in our lives. There are only so many times you can wrestle your child on the front lawn or have the police show up at your door before the neighbors start asking questions. Throw an ambulance in the mix and you really have a show! Luther and I decided early on that public things would be public and private things would be private. If you didn't see it happen or it wasn't in the newspaper or on the Mobile Patrol app (Mobile Patrol: Public Safety, Appriss Insights LLC), it was our battle and not for others to know. Setting these boundaries allowed us to survive the stares, questions and obvious and not-so-obvious whispers.

The most important of these boundaries was putting God first. Allowing Him to hear our sorrows and questions always set us on a path of survival with actual LIFE. A tearful prayer session was often followed by good conversation and laughter over pizza and wings (we are Buffalonians, after all). The all-absorbing nature of addiction tried to and did, for painful stretches, rob us of joy, family, friends and a healthy marriage. We learned that despite what was happening, we needed the Lord to lead us. Otherwise, we were tired and defeated.

Our little family got it wrong plenty of times but we were determined to love Sarah like Christ loved her until somebody's last breath. Trust me, there were days when I begged for the Lord to take me first. The weight was just too heavy. There were days I begged Him to take Sarah. Lord, just please relieve Sarah of her suffering. But each time the Comforter came and sat with me, gave me encouragement through the Word and helped me to persevere for His glory just one more day.

Early in Sarah's drug use we were so overwhelmed that we tried many avenues to get her on the path of recovery. We used every resource available to us—friends, the law, counseling, treatment programs, etc.—but at the end of the day, we just had to release her back to the Lord for His will to be done. As Sarah's dependency on drugs increased, Luther and I grew in dependence on scripture, prayer and wise counsel. As a result, an idea or plan would always emerge to direct our next steps. It was a painful time of learning and listening.

There were plenty of times when we were determined to fulfill our vacation plans or ministry travel regardless of Sarah's condition. Many times we left her homeless or in jail. With God's grace, Sarah's addiction had lost the ability to order our lives. The chains of our bondage to her addiction were broken. It was extraordinarily painful but we slowly learned that the Lord had given us life and we were meant to live it abundantly. When I would sit on a plane asking my husband if we were doing the right thing, he would encourage me that plans could always be changed if something happened or if it was just too difficult. We forced ourselves to enjoy the friends and the beauty around us. Family and friends would sometimes question our plans. We appreciated their input and took their concerns to the Lord. Sometimes it meant we stayed home, yet many times we went. In retrospect every time we left home it was refreshing and fruitful, albeit difficult.

Addiction allowed us to see another side of humility and obedience. Pre-Sarah we were never concerned about arrests or what the justice system looked like. Living outside the law and under the law of grace (Romans 6:14), as Scripture encourages, truly kept us happy yet perhaps a bit naive to other people's struggles with the law. But the Lord loves to teach us how to love the broken and the struggler. He needed Luther and me to experience places that were deeper and darker. Places He prepared and others wouldn't go, called or not. We rejected this "call" for quite a while until we were worn out from resisting. We only found hope when we surrendered and trusted the Lord as we began to serve those lost in addiction. Here, Sarah would be our teacher. And boy, was she an incredible teacher.

The bottom line, Sarah was and is the best person to define her own addiction. The trauma, the bondage and loneliness. I pray that you read her entries with open eyes and an open heart, finding something to learn. Addiction is sneaky and the enemy uses it very effectively to keep believers bound. Is there a way out? Yes, of course. I've seen people completely delivered through a single prayer but most of us travel a long arduous road to freedom. As we learned from our shared experiences with Sarah, the Lord is in both courses.

Scriptures for Consideration

Psalm 143:10 (NKJV) *"Teach me to do Your will, for you are my God; Your Spirit is good. Lead me in the land of uprightness."* (Sarah's choice)

I Corinthians 10:13 (ESV) *"No temptation has overtaken you that is not common to man. God is faithful, and he will not let you be tempted beyond your ability, but with the temptation he will also provide the way of escape, that you may be able to endure it."*

I Corinthians 6:12 (ESV) *"All things are lawful for me, but not all things are helpful. All things are lawful to me, but I will not be dominated by anything."*

James 5:15-16 (NIV) *"And the prayer offered in faith will make the sick person well; the Lord will raise them up. If they have sinned, they will be forgiven. Therefore confess your sins to each other and pray for each other so that you may be healed. The prayer of a righteous person is powerful and effective."*

Romans 5:3-5 (NIV) *"Not only so, we rejoice in our sufferings, knowing that suffering produces endurance, and endurance produces character, and character produces hope, and hope does not put us to shame, because God's love has been poured into our hearts through the Holy Spirit who has been given to us."*

2 Peter 1:3-4 (ESV) *"His divine power has granted to us all things that pertain to life and godliness, through the knowledge of him who called us to his own glory and excellence, by which he has granted to us his precious and very great promises, so that through them you may become partakers of the divine nature, having escaped from the corruption that is in the world because of sinful desires."*

Music to Inspire

"Breaking The Habit," Linkin Park
"Sober" Kelly Clarkson
"I have His Hope," Tenth Avenue North
"Your hands," JJ Heller
"Not Going Back," Hezekiah Walker
"Worth Fighting For," Brian Courtney Wilson
"Gracefully Broken," Tasha Cobbs
"Not an Addict," K's Choice perfectly describes addiction

10 months and always smiling

Sarah and some of her cousins: (Top) Trey, Sarah,
Nick, (Bottom) Tori, Samantha, Julian

Age 2, Silly + Sweet

Confidently Sarah, age 2

Her favorite shades, age 3

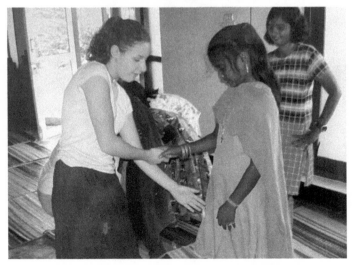

Age 12, Coimbatore, India

Her favorite guy, age 15

Freshman year

Cousin-Sisters, Samantha, Sarah, Tori

A special bond, Sarah and her grandmother

Sarah Louise is with **Luther K** ⋯
Robinson and **Janet Pordon-**
Stasiowski.

Oct 3, 2017 · 👥

My grandparents and parents both are
a striking example to me how to love
unconditionally and fully. Truly blessed
to have the family I do.happy 57th
anniversary to gram n pop and 13th to
my parents 🤍🤍🤍keep shining,you
crazy diamonds 👍🥴

She treasured family

When Sarah didn't respond we searched the internet

Tough yet tender, age 23

Luther & I baptizing Sarah, age 24

Just Sarah, age 24

The last time I saw Sarah alive, June 2020

Chapter 6

Family Matters

*"And may you have the power to understand,
as all God's people should, how wide, how long,
how high, and how deep His love is."*
Ephesians 3:18 (NLT)

June 3, 2017

Riding back to the (Niagara) Falls at 3:05 AM. I feel awfully confused about my life, my goals, especially that I know God has a purpose for me but my master (drugs) has got one helluva stronghold over me. It is really scary. What if I never get another chance to make it back?? I don't want people to remember me as I am now. Lord God I am scared that I will lose this battle. All I want is Jesus but Sarah keeps getting in my way. She is trying to kill me. She wants the enemy to devour my Spirit. And so far she is winning. I know the Lord is more powerful than all things and my addiction is a deception that it is worth giving in to. You are the Alpha and the Omega. Blessed be your name.

I love my mom with all my heart. I never told her that sometimes I just stare at her because she's so beautiful. I admire her spirit and heart so very much and I've just wanted to be like her. She is amazing and fearless.

January 23, 2019

I almost didn't use today. Of course a situation arose with my mom...to where I got so angry I was crying. So then I really showed them by hurting me. Man I can't even get one day clean even on methadone....

I said some very hurtful and ignorant things to my mom today. I am ashamed of myself. Lord please forgive me for my hurtful, bitter, evil, words and behavior towards her. I will do my best to come from a kind, loving and compassionate place in myself. Either that or I will just say nothing.

Spring 2019

Too much crack and dope mixed. Here I sit again writing a goodbye letter just in case it's actually my time...Please God don't let me die like this. I wanted so much more for myself. Mom and Luth you guys are the best. I am so blessed. Never stop laughing. Thank you for showing me what unconditional love is.

March 16, 2019

Tonight was a disaster. Why am I so hard on myself? Really nobody in my life had ever told me I was worthless or a P.O.S or not worth trying. Even (her birth father). The enemy *planted those lies and now they've flourished into full-grown poison ivy. Lord I'm crying out to you, help me surrender fully to You! That I can allow myself to heal. When mom says my healing is going to be slow and steady, like that sh*** scares me!*

I'm so, so, so tired of keeping people at arm's length. I always hurt the people I love the most and I hate that. I love my mom and Luth so much like they are my heroes. But it's like I continue to sh** on them and don't mean to but I want actual fruitful relationships.

June 11, 2019

Today has been so frickin wild. So so strange I don't even know how to explain it. So many emotions yet feeling so weirdly numb. I don't GET IT like what in the actual f*** is wrong with me! Why can't I just get it? I love my family so much, even when I act like an ass. I look up to mom and Luth and G & P so very much. I am so blessed to have such amazing role models in my life and I feel like I just sh** all over all of my blessings. Please forgive me Lord.

June 15, 2019

So today is Saturday and it's been a long day for some reason. I ended up helping my mom though for a while which was really nice. I feel bad though kinda because I asked her if I was gonna get paid. And she said, "What? Get paid to hang out with me??" And I didn't honestly get what we were doing. Like I really thought we were doing like something that I'd get paid for. I feel bad she just wanted to spend time with me. I am so selfish sometimes...

Sarah coveted time with her extended family. As an only child, she needed the sister-love her girl cousins poured on her. Her grandparents near and far loved her and accepted her just as she was. While they always longed for more time with Sarah, they were willing to accept what they got and treasured each moment. They loved patiently and expectantly, like Jesus does. The male cousins treated her like another sibling and that always made her feel loved. They had her back when a boyfriend mistreated her or she put herself in unnecessarily risky situations. Her aunts and uncles were there for her too. Many times they would visit Sarah if she was in a rehab or a sober living home in their area or send her gifts and letters wherever she was. They opened their homes to her frequently. Everyone's investment in Sarah was special because they thought of her as special and she knew it.

Often times Sarah felt unworthy of family love and acted out negatively to sabotage those relationships. The day of my nephew's wedding was the same day as the funeral of her closest friend and on-again/off-again boyfriend who died of complications after a drug overdose at which Sarah was present. While she tried earnestly to convince us she was emotionally well enough to attend the wedding, we knew she was suffering. Her suffering flooded out at the wedding, she got really drunk and her behavioral choices that night alienated her from family and friends. For some, it was their last interaction with Sarah. And while they forgave her, she was unable to gain enough clean time to ask for their forgiveness. Lessons from the grave have taught us to seek forgiveness and resolve issues quickly.

If there is one thing I can say about having a healthy relationship with a loved one in addiction, it is "family matters." It is very easy to allow addiction to define—or redefine—family. After all, stealing and lying don't make for good relational foundations. In and through all our messiness, using Christ's love for us as our example, we chose to love Sarah just as she was, finding something divine in doing so. It was tremendously difficult, but that is what we consciously chose to do.

Jesus speaking to his disciples in John 13:34-35 said, "A new commandment I give to you, that you love one another: [How?] just as I have loved you, you also are to love one another. By this all people will know that you are my disciples, if you have love for one another." His example set the stage to love sacrificially through the power of the Holy Spirit. By freely accepting Christ's love, loving Sarah wasn't an option but a commandment. To be obedient to His commandment, our strength alone was not enough. We needed Christ to show us how to love with His agape or perfect, unconditional, sacrificial and pure love.

I am in no way implying that anyone should accept unacceptable behavior or suffer abuse from a person in addiction. That is not relationship. What I am suggesting is that relational foundations such as mutual respect, communication, support and love remain intact regardless of situation. This is not my novel idea; it's God's. Romans 5:8 states that, "God demonstrates His love toward us, in that while were still sinners, Christ died for us" (NKJV). He draws us near with an everlasting love when we least deserve it to give us hope and a future. This is such a precious reminder that our imperfections do not make us unlovable. Hallelujah! His glory is made manifest as we accept His love, let go of our sinful ways and become more like Him. As we personally and internally learn to accept Christ's love, we can then love others that way too, *even while they're still rebellious*. Not easy, but so worth it.

I am thankful for the part of me that just let Sarah be herself. At her best, she was quirky, artistic, smart and joyful, randomly bursting out in song or a loud "Wheeeeee" for no apparent reason. I learned early on to feed the good parts of her and to pray against the bad. I kept mental notes of the things that didn't seem quite right and sought out wise counsel on how to respond. As hard as I tried, I knew it was not my responsibility to fix Sarah. Support groups like Al-Anon helped give me the tools to let "Sarah be Sarah" and have a sound mind in the face of unending chaos.

Sarah and I had an extraordinary relationship from day one. She was marvelous and I marveled. I listened to advice from other parents and trusted the instincts the Holy Spirit placed in my heart and mind. Yes, we got on each other's nerves, disagreed and fought with each other. There were groundings and other punishments as in any typical household. I would yell, she would slam doors but we would both be laughing by the end of the day. In general, life was good.

Sarah and I developed a secret language of love and understanding from the time she was an infant. She responded to gentle touch and loved to have her hands rubbed. When Sarah was a fussy infant in a car seat, she would reach her tiny hand forward and I would hold it while we drove.

When Sarah was a lonely, moody preteen, she would sit next to me and I would take her hand and massage it, even if she resisted. As a rebellious teen and addicted adult, she would squish herself between Luther and I on the couch and give us each a hand to rub or one person a hand and the other her head to massage. She didn't need to say anything and neither did we. Touch was our language. Touch allowed Sarah's hardened outside to soften and in those moments she knew she was loved beyond her guilt and shame.

During her many hospitalizations for hepatitis C and detoxification, handholding sustained us. Talking about choices and their consequences was exhausting and repetitive. The resolution was always the same, "I'll try harder." Holding hands granted us a little respite from the perpetual storm.

Holding hands however, was not an option when Sarah was incarcerated. Correctional visits consisted of one quick hug, if we were lucky. After that, hands had to remain flat on the counter. This was a very difficult rule to follow because we both talked with our hands; we were reprimanded frequently. Oops. We often giggled at the completely ridiculous nature of the situations in which we found ourselves; at other times we silently stared at each other's hands dreaming of that healing touch.

On the flip side, Luther and I spent significant time developing safe boundaries to ensure that Sarah could not take advantage of these gentle touches or kind words. Mark Gregston, founder of Heartlight Ministries and author of "Parenting Today's Teens," compares developing healthy boundaries to raising horses. Inside the fence the horse has everything it needs: food, shelter and room for movement and testing the boundaries. The corral needs to be a safe place for a horse to be trained, but not broken. If the horse finds its way out of the corral then the fence needs to be repaired. Importantly, the rancher determines where the fence posts are set. I probably mangled his analogy, but we loved what it meant for us. Sarah, Luther and I developed healthy, clear boundaries and consequences that kept our relationship open even if it meant Sarah could no longer live in our house and "feed in our pasture."

A practical tool from Heartlight Ministries to help us develop respectful and practical boundaries was the family belief system. (Free e-book on heartlightministries.org/developing-rules-and-consequences-offer). This worksheet prompted us to identify up to 10 beliefs that we all agreed were important in our home. Some of ours included being treated with respect, honesty at all costs and healthy living (e.g., no smoking, drugs or alcohol). We each agreed on the level of consequence when the belief system was broken.

During her teen years this signed and dated document hung on the refrigerator and was updated as needed with enhanced beliefs or differing consequences as needed. The result of applying this chart was that it literally took the fight out of discipline. When Sarah got angry because of a consequence, it was of her own making and she knew it…and hated it. What it meant for us was that the refrigerator took most of the abuse and not us. When she would ask us to go somewhere or do something that was clearly not on our belief system, I would tell her to check the list first and make her own decision. As she went to the refrigerator, I would make myself busy in another room and listen at a safe distance for the inevitable grumbling. Ironically, as rebellious as Sarah was, she routinely accepted these self-imposed consequences and many potentially volatile situations were avoided. There were times when the consequences of our family belief system had to be handled by law enforcement, but because it was always listed on the sheet as a consequence, Sarah was never surprised. I believe the implementation of this tool helped save our relationship regardless of the severity of the consequence.

We adopted a similar approach for the numerous times Sarah unsuccessfully lived with us as an adult. The consequence list just wasn't on the fridge anymore. Copies were posted in our rooms. The belief system chart made life much easier as we waded through unfamiliar waters, especially when we had to ask her to leave.

When Sarah was about 17, we developed an "honesty at all costs" truce. I found I could deal with almost anything as long as I knew what was real. Sarah's continued desire for close family ties meant that, to the best of her ability, she would tell us where she was in her addiction and depression. Sarah was also the absolute worst liar and she knew it too. Sometimes we confronted her and sometimes we just took note. Many times I would simply repeat back to her whatever nonsense came out of her mouth. We would look at each other, she'd try to stare me down and then we would just burst out laughing. You really want to go with that story?? Okay, Louie Lou (as we often called her), let's go with that. Eye roll. Despite the attempted lies and the difficult-to-accept truths, Luther, Sarah and I benefited in unimaginable ways from our "honesty at all costs" policy. Instead of division our bond grew tighter.

I have to repeat that the gift of laughter was an incredible blessing to us. We loved to laugh. Odd movies, Luther's ridiculous jokes or the improper use of a word would send us into gales of laughter, often at inappropriate times. And if you added in any member of our entire extended family to these moments, it was usually sidesplitting. We all came by the gift of laughter honestly.

There were knock-down-drag-out fights—primarily verbal—but those were few and far between. Physical confrontations were primarily restricted to those times when we had to restrain Sarah for her own protection while under the influence. One of the last times I physically confronted her, I didn't realize she was self-detoxing and in a very paranoid state. Sarah was threateningly close to me and after yelling for her to back up, I pushed her arm. She quietly backed up and when I turned back around she punched me in the face. I stood there stunned and in excruciating pain. Sarah looked at me in shock and immediately packed her bags, knowing she had crossed the line. In our ten-year addiction journey, this was the only time I was glad to see her go. What Sarah and I learned from my physical and emotional pain and her remorse and shame was enough to change the manner in which we interacted from that day forward, regardless of her mental state.

Even as we watched Sarah nearing the end of her battle with addiction, we vowed that every moment we had together would be filled with honesty and as much joy and laughter as we could muster. Sarah had a contagious laugh. It was like an embarrassed roll of high-pitched giggles. Anyone who heard it would just start laughing, too. While we took very seriously every arrest, hospitalization and misdeed, those were hers to own. Our job was to treasure each and every moment we had together.

It often took people by surprise that despite incarceration, overdoses and repeated stays at rehabs, we still had joy. In our rehab counseling sessions (there were over 42, remember) the counselors would ask the same family trauma questions or insinuate that there were unresolved issues in our relationship. Sarah would politely say, "It's not them. It's not us. It's me and my addiction." One time, we had a counselor who stopped the session and just stared at us, finally saying, "I have never seen a family like yours. You guys really love each other!" Thank you for noticing!

It all sounds depressing and perhaps a bit bizarre, but we really did cherish every opportunity to be together even if it wasn't perfect. Once, she was living in her car in a parking lot in Maryland. When I came into town, Sarah invited me to her car for a visit. "Would you like to sit in the back seat or the front?"…as if this were a perfectly natural situation. We would talk, listen to music or eat a snack. We knew that this season would end with another detox stint, arrest or death so we were determined to spend time together without highlighting the obvious.

Normalcy was something Sarah deeply desired. Her lifestyle was anything but normal and our worlds often collided. The irony of what she wanted and what she did challenged us deeply to respond lovingly and without judgment. We often bit our tongues and adjusted our actions because she simply couldn't do either.

We established communication rules that could not be violated because family mattered deeply to each of us. Sarah lived dangerously yet still Luther and I still needed some level of contact with her. The three of us made an agreement that whenever she was on a bender Sarah would have to call me every other day. If the third day came and I didn't hear from her, I would text or call her. If she didn't respond within two hours, we agreed that I would call the police or locate her myself. In her 10 years of addiction, this only happened two or three times. When I did locate Sarah, sometimes she would come home with me and sometimes she chose to stay where she was. At least I had seen her and knew she was alive. Never okay, just alive. Sarah longed for our relationship as much as we did. In her addiction, she had lost just about everything and we were not going to allow her to lose her family, too. It wasn't easy or pretty, but it was worth it.

Scriptures for Consideration

I Corinthians 13:4-8 (TPT) *"Love is large and incredibly patient. Love is gentle and consistently kind to all. It refuses to be jealous when blessing comes to someone else. Love does not brag about one's achievements nor inflate its own importance. Love does not traffic in shame and disrespect, nor selfishly seek its own honor. Love is not easily irritated or quick to take offense. Love joy-fully celebrates honesty and finds no delight in what is wrong. Love is a safe place of shelter, for it never stops believing the best for others. Love never takes failure as defeat, for it never gives up."*

Psalm 133:1 (GNT) *"How good and pleasant it is when God's people live together in unity!"*

Romans 12:9 (ESV) *"Let love be genuine. Abhor what is evil; hold fast to what is good."*

I John 4:19 (NASB) *"We love because He first loved us."*

I Corinthians 13:13 (ESV) *"So now faith, hope and love abide, these three; but the greatest of these is love."*

Ephesians 3:18 (NLT) *"And may you have the power to understand, as all God's people should, how wide, how long, how high, and how deep His love is."* (Sarah's Choice)

I John 2:9 (NKJV) *"He who says he is in the light, and hates his brother, is in darkness until now. He who loves his brother, abides in the light and there is no cause for stumbling in him."* (Sarah's Choice)

Music to Inspire

"This is not Your Legacy," Matthew West
"Always," Seventh Day Slumber
"Psalm 23 (I am not alone)," Josh Sherman
"One Thing Remains," Jesus Culture
"We Are Family," Sister Sledge

Chapter 7

Unlikely Resources

"Do not be wise in your own eyes,
Fear the Lord and depart from evil. It will be health
to your flesh, And strength to your bones."
Proverbs 3:7 (KJV)

The following is a glimpse into Sarah's 12 Step recovery homework assigned by her Narcotics Anonymous sponsor.

2018

The 1st Step Promises?
 -discover the fatal nature of our disease
 -become opened minded to conviction
 -be willing to listen

Step 1 "We admitted that we were powerless over our addic-
tion, that our lives had become unmanageable

-My life is still unmanageable because I'm in another program that I hate. My mom is holding the majority of my finances at the moment because I have no idea how to handle that amount of money (gifted to Sarah by her paternal grandfather). I am so awkward in my skin and trust myself so little that I feel like I need to run every decision by somebody because I'm terrified to do something so wrong thus making myself feel a certain way pushing me to use, which sounds dumb even on paper-but basically my life is still unmanageable because I don't know how to do life things without a lot of extra help.

-I am powerless over just about everything in my life. Being powerless over drugs and alcohol doesn't always cause me distress. That one is pretty easy for me to accept most days. Other things that are harder for me once the drugs are gone is that I'm powerless over people. Sometimes I'm powerless over my reactions-which is really the only thing I do have power over but sometimes I even fail to control that. Presently I'm powerless over location and being able to be able to walk away from people and go somewhere and that's distressing.

-I don't think powerlessness is a particularly negative thing. I believe the more I accept how little control I have over most things the more positive experience or at least the more "ok" I feel about it...The more I accept it the better I can see the positive side of me taking my hands off the wheel.

-Surrendering can sometimes be labeled or connoted as bad but to me it means that I've just given up fighting something that is going to beat my butt over time.

-Vulnerability always seemed like a weakness to me because I have always felt like I had to uphold the tough guy exterior-I was a fraud and I now feel like being vulnerable is not weak-in fact I feel that it is incredibly courageous. It still makes me incredibly uncomfortable. I suspect the more I do it and allow people to see me for me, the more I will see it as a strength.

Step 2: "We came to believe that a power greater than ourselves could restore us to sanity"

-What makes me feel close to God-praying, church, helping others, being in meetings (sometimes) identifying with other addicts, connecting with others, connecting with myself (When I can be ok being alone with myself and my head isn't a mess), music.

-I don't have any hang-ups with God. Yes, I believe in God. I believe I can be restored to sanity, but it will be a long slow process I'm learning, which is ok because I feel like no human is ever 100% sane.

-I have come to find out that although I've always had unshakeable faith in the power of God, that in no way substitutes a relationship with Him and I would wonder why my faith wasn't changing my use or even I would get sober and my addictive behaviors would get really bad and I'm all high and mighty because I'm a Christian and have great faith. Well I wasn't actively working on a relationship with Him or even if I was trying to, I would like pick and choose what spiritual principles to act out; like treating others with love or not tearing people apart with words or talking crap on someone when I know I've done the same thing. Now I'm taking action and being or trying anyway to be more proactive on living right even behind closed doors.

I have always loved the underdog and the troubled kid. Their angst is honest and in my years as a church youth director, their behavior pushed me to love differently. I had to allow them grace when they didn't know church etiquette and speak rather bluntly when their behavior was out of control. I adored these kids. They were deep thinkers, raw, sometimes honest; like seeds pushing through the hardened ground. That said, I don't EVER remember asking the Lord for a troubled child of my own. Sarah took that job seriously and to a whole new level. We had to learn quickly what we could and couldn't do to offer her help. It was a 24/7 job and we were constantly waiting for the other shoe to drop.

Sarah would often tell us prior to and throughout her addiction that she felt like her brain didn't work properly. Since she had already been diagnosed as having clinical depression, we took her concerns seriously and had a neuropsychological evaluation completed. The evaluation concluded that Sarah was an intelligent girl with depression, drug-induced anxiety and slight deficiencies in math. In theory, these were all diagnoses that could be worked through with the proper interventions.

We leaned into trusted family and friends for clues on where to get help for her and support for ourselves. Whether they could suggest resources or not, they always agreed to pray fervently. We had (and still do have) the best prayer team this side of heaven. I could text, call or show up at any hour of the day or night, unannounced and my saints would listen, research and pray with me on Sarah's behalf. Together, we hit lots of dead-ends but also found resources that were worth a try.

As mentioned earlier, one of those resources was Heartlight Ministries in Texas. At that time, our concern was that Sarah's behavior was riskier than that of the average partying teen. By then we had tried counseling, scholastic interventions and switching high schools, all to no avail. The saying, "you can lead a horse to water but you can't make it drink," was true beyond words.

Before we sent Sarah to Heartlight, she adamantly refused our attempts at local residential placements. We continued to warn her that at some point it would no longer be her choice. As things escalated, we took drastic measures and had her involuntarily transported to the Texas program. This was a source of hurt for Sarah for a long time, but as parents we truly believed there were no other residential options from which she wouldn't leave. To our grateful surprise, she thrived in this program. Sarah would never have chosen it, but there she began to discover who she was. She eventually thanked us for sending her to Heartlight, but that gratitude was years in the making.

After completing eight months of the twelve-month program, it was no longer financially feasible to keep Sarah at Heartlight and we made the difficult decision to bring her home. One of the problems with addiction is that it forces many decisions to be made on the spur of the moment, making it easy to get in over one's head. Luther and I came to the realization that allowing one member of the family to dominate our time, energy and finances was not sustainable. In addition, our local school district had offered Sarah creative resources to allow her to graduate with her class. At the time, bringing her home seemed like a logical choice for all of us. In hindsight we should have found a way for her to complete Heartlight, even if it meant Sarah would not graduate on time. The inability to complete programs or "anything," for that matter, was a source of constant sadness and regret for Sarah. We understood later that every unfinished venture added to her sense of failure and negative self-image.

Upon her return to Buffalo, we had a short period of normalcy at home and school. But Sarah soon became bored and slowly amassed an eclectic group of people who seemed fun-loving and lived on the edge. Later, she told us how much inner turmoil she had about hanging out with these "friends" as she knew it was against everything she had learned and experienced during the past year. However, that conviction was not enough to stop her risk-taking activities; Sarah was confident that she could move past her destructive behaviors and still be with this group. She was very wrong. The allure of the activities of this group became harder to resist and soon they all began using drugs intravenously. Sarah later told me she was really afraid and that she intended to use just once and then divorce herself from these "friends." That "one time use" changed Sarah from being a rebellious youth to living an instant life of addiction. With that singular action, normalcy ceased and years of compromised living began.

In the early years, Sarah's drug use and illegal behaviors were done in secret and Luther and I had no idea of the extent of her problems. We continued to encourage Sarah to address her mental health concerns through medication and counseling as well as avoiding people who were using drugs. (It all sounds so naive now.)

Sarah graduated from high school early and started cosmetology school at 17 years of age. She appeared to be thriving until one day her instructor called to tell me that Sarah was excessively sleepy during class and asked me if she had any health concerns. A week or so earlier, I had suspected she was using drugs again due to a few odd behaviors. Sarah and I discussed my concerns and she assured me she was clean. I further dismissed that thought as she was making friends at school, got a job and appeared more positive than I had seen her in a long time. Nevertheless and just to be sure she was not using, I searched her room and found a shoe filled with orange caps from used syringes. My stomach sank. I called the director back and asked if they had a policy in place for drug use on campus or if they had a NARCAN® kit. The answer was "no" to both questions. Sarah couldn't be expelled because there was no policy and she hadn't been caught using drugs on campus. I copied relevant addiction materials and encouraged the cosmetology school to develop a policy quickly and become NARCAN® trained. The director gave her a warning but within several months Sarah had her first arrest for possession of illegal drugs. Cosmetology school was over.

From that first arrest and for the next few years, we learned the jail phone system, visiting rules, court lingo and how to use the Mobile Patrol app. I asked the Lord a million times, "Why is this happening?" But because I'm rather pragmatic, the answer was obvious. I changed my question to, "What now, Lord?" I became a student of the systems. I watched, listened and learned from my seat in the courtroom, the ER waiting room and during residential placement counseling sessions.

Each time Sarah was arrested, I saw my beautiful daughter shackled, without undergarments, matted unkempt hair, withdrawing, walking down the court building hallways to sit in the courtroom, debased by her own actions. Fortunately, Buffalo has drug court in which low-level offenders are offered recovery interventions as an alternative and deterrent to long-term incarceration. As we navigated these systems, I saw many people who cared deeply for the affairs of the downtrodden. Court officers would whisper to Sarah, "You don't belong here" followed by words of encouragement. The staff of drug court worked tirelessly to ensure participant's rights were not violated and that appropriate help was offered. Judges spoke respectfully and offered mercy. And while society loves to speak negatively of the police, the majority of the law enforcement officers we encountered did exactly what they were trained to do. Sometimes it's just the system that's broken. In so many instances, they offered her another chance, leading me to pray for the court staff and participants (I still do). These unsung heroes have a thankless job.

In most cases, I was the only family member to be present for a defendant's court appearance. I tried to never interfere with a fair amount of success; Sarah either had to pay the consequences for her actions or get the help she needed. My primary position was to advocate for her and assist with transportation if needed. When she would refuse treatment, she would be sent back to jail for more time to weigh her options or serve her sentence. The next time Sarah would appear before the judge, I would be there, positioned so she could see me, and she would look for me to give me the usual scowl. I would look back at her with my "I can't fix this, but I love you" look which she well understood. The responsibility of being Sarah's parent weighed heavily, but it was a yoke of love.

Early in her use, we were advised by many to avoid the legal system. "It will be hard for her to get a job with a record." "She'll only get more illegal contacts or learn more negative behaviors." For the most part, this did not turn out to be true. We were incredibly grateful for "the system." Drug courts and jail kept Sarah alive longer than the streets ever would have. I take my hat off to the officers that have to do strip searches, get spit on, watch people withdraw, clean up vomit, get called expletives and watch someone take a urine test all day long. I am eternally grateful for their work.

Another hidden blessing of the drug court was that programs like intensive outpatient treatment and recovery groups were mandated. These mandates made Sarah eligible for Medicaid that, in turn, paid for the copays our private insurance didn't cover. In addition, the staff of drug court would set up the initial appointments or find available inpatient treatment beds and even at times provide transportation. The benefits of drug court were numerous and allowed Sarah to be directly involved and responsible for her own recovery.

Sarah failed miserably in drug court. She entered over 42 detoxes or recovery programs. Her greatest regret in her own words, was that she only "lived well in captivity." After two-to-three years, she pleaded out of drug court and accepted the sentence of four to six months in jail with misdemeanor drug charges on her record. Ironically, there was so much peace within her during that period of incarceration. She requested books of historical biblical fiction and read everything she could get her hands on. Amazon Prime made regular deliveries to the correctional facility. Our visits and telephone calls were mostly positive. Jail phone time is expensive so if Sarah was cranky or belligerent, a "bye-bye" on our end was quick to come. We both developed new, healthy communication boundaries that helped us adapt to these challenging situations. Mine included a limit to the amount of money I would spend on books or commissary, one weekly visit and respectful speech during all of our contact. Sarah had to limit her phone conversations so that money was not wasted on chitchat. She could only request books that were positive (no serial killer books) and politely stop me if I asked questions that were too painful or triggering.

I have great respect for the fellow families who sat next to me for hours waiting to visit their incarcerated loved one. Race, education or socioeconomic status didn't matter. The same rules applied to everyone. No exceptions. On one visit, I was in a rush to get in line and wore an underwire bra (not allowed). I didn't realize it until my number was called to go through the series of locked doors and the metal detector went off. The guard said, "Ma'am, you have five minutes to decide what you want to do." My options were ditch the bra and wear a sheer shirt while walking through a waiting room full of people followed by prison guards and inmates or not visit. "Lord, is this really happening?" Sarah had called me hysterical the night before and was desperate for a visit. It would take me too long to run to my car for the "prison wear" I kept in my trunk. Wasting precious minutes, I went into the bathroom and cried. A much larger woman came out of the stall, saw my face and said, "Underwire?" I nodded. She said, "Want my camisole?" Overwhelmed, I nodded yes. "Pass it on to the next person who needs it." This woman literally gave me the shirt off her back. I was so grateful. I quickly wrapped the camisole around me three times for a tad bit of modesty and ran back in line. The guards thought for certain I had left. The Lord IS near to the broken hearted.

We had many prison visits; some were sad and others were hysterically funny. Sarah was a good storyteller and the stuff that happens in jail you just can't make up. It's hard to laugh with your hands on a table as the guards stare you down. Sometimes during our visits we just cried and spoke from the heart. Each time, we prayed. Whether we were laughing or crying, we were always a spectacle and, I pray, a good witness too! One of the major life lessons I gained during these years of experiences is that we are all guilty of something and there are consequences to our actions; to love and be loved must always be our top priority.

The emergency room was another one of those places where love had to triumph over feelings. I spent many nights accompanying Sarah to the emergency room to be admitted into detox. If you've ever gone to a county hospital waiting room at night, you will understand that this is no ordinary place. There are people from all walks of life and with all kinds of problems. Some people were homeless and killing time; others were in serious need of medical help.

On one notable occasion, Sarah's doctor had prescribed naltrexone, a medical intervention to help prevent chronic relapses. It is a drug that blocks the effects of opioids and at the same time causes significant adverse side effects if an opioid is used before starting the medication. I knew she was actively using and told her not to take the naltrexone. She was disgusted with my lack of trust in her and took the pill. Within minutes, she dropped to the floor with severe muscle cramps. With all the self-control I could muster, I stepped over her writhing body and said, "Hmm…I thought you weren't using."

Off we went to the ER, with Sarah in the backseat thrashing like a caged animal. We arrived and waited for what seemed like an eternity. I sat there, forcing myself to calmly read a book while Sarah pounded her legs trying to ease the muscle cramps. She looked possessed. Perhaps she was. Either way, we needed to stay and seek help. It took two days to get her symptoms under control and as soon as she was released from the hospital she was back using heroin again. This time, homeless. But whenever she called and wanted to go to the ER with the intentions of detox, Luther and I didn't hesitate to take her or drop her off.

Life was generally intense, but there were moments of humor. At one point in her homelessness, Sarah was in desperate need of detox. She sneaked home and stole one of our cars (that is not the funny part). We called her phone and she told us that she was going to the hospital and we could find our car there. Off to the hospital we raced. As we drove into the parking lot, we were passed by a man driving our car. Luther did a 180 and chased after him. As the man stopped at a signal, we swerved in front of him, blocking his way forward. Luther jumped out of the car, ran toward the man and screamed, "Get out of our car!" The frightened young man looked up at Luther and said he was merely parking it. "Oh no, you're not! Give me the keys!" Luther demanded. It was only as the poor guy stepped out of the car that we saw the word "Valet" on his jacket. Oops! Super humbled, we thanked him and gave him a vague explanation for Luther's behavior. The man laughed nervously and proceeded to park our car, frequently checking the rearview mirror to see if we were following him. It was a moment of dark humor but we had to laugh at ourselves and also at the fact that Sarah was so desperate for detox that she employed valet parking. Rest assured, the young man was tipped handsomely.

The hospital continued to be a generally good source of intervention for Sarah. During one admission, after being revived from an overdose, Sarah refused inpatient substance abuse treatment and wanted to be released. As the staff was preparing her discharge papers, I privately informed them that she had an outstanding warrant and needed to be taken directly to jail once she was released. If not taken into custody, Sarah would be back again and perhaps not so fortunate the next time. Not one medical professional followed through and one nurse told me that I wasn't being very compassionate. I called the hospital police myself and insisted they arrest Sarah. They did. She was infuriated. And yes, I was in drug court the next day to show support.

Unfortunately, one can't be forced to go to treatment. No matter how hard the doctors may try, they can't keep patients against their will. I learned to aptly use the phrase, "she is a danger to herself and others," as a means to either have her arrested or kept for observation. I hoped that with a little medical relief, Sarah would be able to think clearly enough to choose treatment again. It was the best and perhaps only phrase that prompted immediate police or medical intervention.

Warrants can be a life saving tool. When Sarah was under 21 and legally in our care, there were few obstacles to having her arrested. Over 21, our only recourse was to call in her warrants and hope the police would pick her up. The last time Sarah was arrested, she was living at home. We knew that her addiction had brought her to her lowest point and we did not want to find her dead body in a trap house or on the streets. She couldn't get out of bed for days at a time, barely showered and never socialized. She was simply existing and not even doing that well. No amount of cajoling or inspirational speeches could rouse her. I pleaded, "Lord, she just can't lie here and die. What do I do?"

About a week into this behavior, I did some investigation and discovered Sarah had an outstanding warrant and I called it in. The police asked if she was being violent, threatening or causing problems. No, I replied. They were confused as to why I would call in her warrant. I simply told them that if they didn't arrest her today, she would die. The police showed up at our house an hour later. They were very professional but asked me again if I really wanted her arrested. Yes; she has a warrant, please arrest her. And so they went upstairs, made sure she was dressed appropriately and took her to the holding center. She did not resist. I did not get any pleasure out of these arrests, but warrants were a resource I was willing to use to give her every opportunity to live free of drugs.

Sarah had many health-related issues as a result of her drug use. She was hospitalized twice for hepatitis C with dangerously elevated liver enzymes. Instead of taking the opportunity to heal, she had her dealer bring her drugs to put in her IV. To anyone else this would be insanity. But to her, it was necessity. The real insanity is that she was never caught. The medical system is designed to treat the primary issue, which in this case hepatitis C, and not look at the whole person. Even armed with full knowledge of her drug history and having to fax drug court daily, not one medical provider drug tested Sarah in the hospital. Not once, not ever.

Drug testing wouldn't have changed her immediate diagnosis, but the lack of testing did identify a clear gap in communication between the medical and judicial systems. While the medical system fulfilled the requirements of drug court by providing the proper paperwork of her admission and discharge, drug court could have or should have requested a toxicology screen during her hospitalization. It would have been a learning opportunity for the medical staff and yet another intervention opportunity for Sarah. This truly would have embraced client-centered treatment. As it was, Sarah was released from the hospital, returned to drug court and outpatient treatment with a physician's note to say she had been hospitalized. There was no positive toxicology screen and therefore no subsequent jail time or intervention.

Not every system we accessed was helpful. Unfortunately, our experience with the substance abuse rehabilitation system was terrible. There were many good counselors who made a positive impact on Sarah and their other clients, but most were stuck working in antiquated systems driven by outdated protocols or insurance limitations. Many of the approaches used in the rehabilitation programs were "cookie cutter" therapies that fulfilled requirements for the facilities versus meeting the more holistic needs of the clients. Sarah was repeatedly left to attend substance abuse counseling that did not and could not address her mental health needs. The system expected a broken, addicted person to attend multiple therapies and to be transparent with each provider. Being truthful is difficult enough once, but sharing your heart over and over is nearly impossible for someone contemplating recovery or in early recovery. Even as these models have been updated, most agencies still use old strategies but under a new name. I was often asked to serve on committees to address these issues but I had little energy left to advocate for better programming. I had to use my energy to help my child.

As with most people who struggle with addiction, Sarah was frequently noncompliant and afraid to attend counseling or groups because her toxicology screens were positive meaning more jail time. It was a vicious cycle. We were grateful for the few service providers who looked out for her each time she came back through the system. One particular counselor called me every few months to see if Sarah was okay even when she was no longer a participant in her program. She saw both Sarah's conflict and worth and was committed to offering her whatever assistance Sarah would accept. What a blessing. When Sarah died, I was overwhelmed by people like this counselor and others from various other programs and courts that called to offer their condolences or attended her memorial service. They all saw a light in Sarah that burned above and through her addiction.

Recovery coaches and peer advocates are the newest resources available. They have a unique role to support a person from contemplating sobriety to recovery. They are a benefit to the new face of recovery. During one sober period, Sarah and I took the recovery coaching course. Halfway through the second session, she relapsed. She came to training as high as a kite and none of the trainers or the participants that day realized it. I was disappointed with their naiveté and equally angry for her disrespect of the course and those in it. Not surprisingly, Sarah maintained that she had used only one time and asked to finish the course and permission was granted.

Even impaired, Sarah's input was invaluable to the other trainees. She was asked deep and personal questions which she answered with complete transparency. I learned a few things, too. She almost finished the course but on the second last day never showed up. At that point, I released her to the Lord (again) and finished the day's training. Later that night, Sarah called to let me know that she had overdosed and had been hospitalized.

The next day, the class was stunned to learn of her overdose. Sarah showed them the very nature of addiction. It was as real as it got.

Christian prayer and deliverance ministries were another important treatment resource. Sarah went through wonderful deliverance ministries, one inpatient and one outpatient. Sarah, Luther and I firmly believed in using the power of the Holy Spirit to heal, deliver and set free. Sarah was terrified to live life without drugs. Everything outside of drug use, even surrendering to the Lord, was overwhelming or foreign to her. Sarah's fear and shame held her captive when the Lord just needed her to come as she was, trusting that He would do everything she couldn't do and more.

One of the best deliverance ministries ever established was started in 1935 by a man named Bill Wilson who talked to his friend Bob Smith about the nature of alcoholism and a possible solution. So began Alcohol Anonymous (AA) and subsequently Narcotics Anonymous (NA). The 12 steps and traditions of the program allow a person seeking abstinence from substances the freedom to explore and engage in recovery anonymously.

I first encountered these recovery rooms (groups) when Sarah's father went to rehab. Having grown up in a Christian home, I struggled a bit with the term "a higher power," because scripture never addresses God as such. But desperate for help, I continued to attend Al-Anon, worked the steps and found that the program was not bound by terminology. I could freely refer to my higher power as God. In these rooms I drew closer to God, not farther away as many people feared. The 12 Steps have been adapted by many other programs and continue to offer countless others freedom from their addictions. What a blessing that Bill W., as he is widely known, had the obedience to follow the leading of the Holy Spirit.

Sponsors and home groups are two of the greatest gifts of AA's program. Isolation is a demon that waits to seize hold of and defeat those in addiction. A sponsor, along with an accessible group of people, can defeat this enemy. You may not resonate with all of the people in a group but slogans like "principles above personalities" and "it works, if you work it" help to develop community that is essential to overcoming addiction. Sarah had incredible support people in her life from AA and NA. Her sponsors gave her tough love. Her program friends patiently waited for her to reach out and engage with them. In reading Sarah's writings, this inability to engage is perhaps the most difficult to see knowing that her help was right there but that for some reason she couldn't, or wouldn't, access it.

I don't know what it's like to be that bound and it seems too easy as a bystander to think we have all the answers. One thing I know for certain is that Sarah really tried to recover. She tried with every fiber of her being so many times. Ultimately, the only thing she never gave up on was God. She loved the Lord and He had mercy on her. That relationship would bring her the final victory.

The services that are featured in this chapter are not the only resources that can be accessed to help your addicted loved one. I have only shared a few that we tried and that worked best for us. If you find something new, try it! You have absolutely nothing to lose. I often felt like a fish out of water, calling places and not knowing the proper terminology or even which services to ask for, but I persisted and I learned. I tripped over my words, I got hung up on and I kept trying. You probably will experience similar scenarios and that is to be expected. Just keep trying.

Scriptures for Consideration

Proverbs 3:7 (KJV) *"Do not be wise in your own eyes, Fear the Lord and depart from evil. It will be health to your flesh, And strength to your bones."* *(Sarah's Choice)*

Proverbs 11:14 (KJV) *"Where no counsel is, the people fall: but in the multitude of counselors there is safety."*

Proverbs 15:22 (GWT) *"Without advice plans go wrong, but with many advisers they succeed."*

Proverbs 20:18 (NLT) *"Plans succeed through good counsel; don't go to war without wise advice."*

Proverbs 16:9 (ESV) *"The heart of man plans his way, but the Lord establishes his steps."*

Romans 12:5 (GNT) *"In the same way, even though we are many individuals, Christ makes us one body and individuals who are connected to each other."*

Music to Inspire

"Don't Do It Without Me," Bishop Paul Morton
"The More I Seek You," Kari Jobe
"Above All," Lenny LeBlanc
"10,000 Reasons", Matt Redman
"I'm Reaching Out," Tommy Walker

Chapter 8

Loss, Grief and Forgiveness

"My flesh and my heart may fail, but God is the strength of my heart and my portion forever."
Psalm 73:26 (NIV)

July 2, 2018

Sunday, the pastor's sermon was basically about wolf and sheep and what to look for in people. See, it was a good warning and everything...But what happens when I identify more as a wolf than a sheep? I know I am still a sheep underneath everything. I hate how I am when I am not clean. I literally have no idea who I am. Besides being manipulative, selfish and numb. I am stuck in survivor mode. Survivor mode revolves around me, and that is the total of my personality right now.

2019 or 2020

Grief & Loss:

Biggest and most recent: [she names her best friend/ boyfriend who died]

Friendships: My old best friend KG, the best friend I ever had. The closest and most open I had ever been to another human being. I started using in our shared apartment and became a very sick individual and horrible friend. She stayed clean and is still sober today. I gave up that relationship for drugs.

Loss of my freedom: Not only due to various legal issues, but not being able to accomplish much and had very little successes with jobs etc. because I'm always sick and preoccupied with getting, using and finding ways and means to get more. I can never go on vacations or always try and get out of visiting family out of town for the fear of going into withdrawal and being a miserable b.

Loss of self-respect: Over the years I've done a lot of immoral acts in the name of money and drugs. Stealing, lying, manipulating, settling and selling myself are just some examples of ways, slowly over time I lost pieces of my morality and self-respect.

(No date)

Dear Sarah,

My girl. We've been through a lot over the years. A lot of good but, also a lot of bad and destruction. I'm writing to sincerely apologize for everything I've ever done to you mind, body and soul. I've continuously put you down, told you that you would never amount to anything, and let others do the same until you wholeheartedly believed it. Not to mention the grotesque marks I've told you were okay to puncture your body with. I'm so sorry that I let you think that your body was your identity and then went as far as rationalizing the irrational sexual encounters, all in the name of, "a good time." I'm sorry for allowing you to lose all faith in anything you ever believed in. Even after I realized the drugs I was putting into you broke your once lively spirit, I continued to tell you it was ok to do these things.

I want to apologize for everything I told you was ok to steal from your greatest support network. None of it was all right. It's not too late to repair though, always remember that.

Love,
Sarah

Somewhere amidst all the chaos of addiction Sarah, Luther and I were grieving. Heavily. We were grieving for the things that had happened and for the things that would never happen. But processing our losses and grief in a healthy way either couldn't happen or occurred in dribs and drabs. There just wasn't much time in active addiction to be introspective. We were too busy surviving.

I mourned the loss of "the normal" and often felt distanced from those who had typical teen milestones to celebrate. Sarah never went to a prom. She never participated in her high school graduation. She never went to college, never got married, never had children and the list goes on. While we did have a pseudo-prom night and a small graduation party for Sarah, the three of us were not invited to the celebrations of others. The parties came and went and we felt the sting of exclusion. Luther and I wanted to share in the celebrations of the children Sarah grew up with. We had grown to love those kids. We actually *needed* to attend, as much as it would have hurt us. And although Sarah may never have attended a graduation party had she been invited, she desperately wanted to be included. And so we all grieved in our own way. Sometimes in denial, pretending we didn't know about events, and sometimes making a healthy effort to do something else, just for us.

At some point, we stopped trying to put ourselves in the "normal family" category. When the children of our friends went off to college, our child went off to jail…or rehab…or to somewhere we didn't know. We learned to stay to ourselves or to be with other people who were on the same journey or who would try to understand our path. It was easier that way and anything easy was a relief.

Communication & Understanding

Luther and I were intentional about not hiding and going about our daily business, but it was stressful, to say the least. Awkward interactions at the grocery store were the worst. I learned to just say hello and keep it moving until the inevitable, "How's Sarah?" My usual answer was, "Still breathing!" in my most chipper voice. It was the most honest answer I could muster. In truth, most people didn't know what to ask and were simply being polite in a casual situation. Because there was nothing casual about our situation, I couldn't answer from that same polite space and sometimes, to my shame (and dark sense of humor), I may have been too honest or embellished a little too much in conversations like this one:

"Hi," says the other person.
"Hi," says me.
"Nice to see you."
"And you."
"How's Sarah?"
"In jail." Awkward silence. "See you later!"

When all Sarah's peers were graduating college and starting glorious new careers and Sarah was between rehab placements, someone inevitably walked into my grief. Here's how that looked:

"Hi," says other person.
"Hi," says me. "How's the family?"
"Good and yours? How's Sarah?"
"Oh, she's working for TripAdvisor."
"Really? That's fantastic. What does she do for them?"

"She's evaluating rehabs up and down the East Coast. Sometimes as far as Texas."

"Wow. I didn't know TripAdvisor did that."

"They don't."

The kind of conversation that always stabbed my heart most was:

"How's Sarah?"

"Still breathing."

"I pray for her everyday. Tell her I'm thinking of her."

"Thank you. I think she would really love to hear from you. Would you like her phone number or address?"

"Um, not right now. I'll call you for it." or "Oh, I don't know her that well. It might be weird."

Casual conversations were just not up to the task of addressing the tender issues at hand.

The "I really feel called to visit Sarah in jail" line always hit hard. Having a child with an addiction that involved shameful behavior was emotionally very difficult. Empty promises only heaped more disappointment and hurt on our already broken hearts. Visiting someone in jail is a huge investment of time and emotional energy so when people expressed interest in visiting Sarah it was difficult not to get our hopes up. For Sarah, it would have meant a lot to have a visit from someone other than Luther and me. We were all hungry for companionship with people that cared deeply and authentically even if they didn't understand addictions.

Prayer & Relationships

Prayer for a person struggling with addiction is vital. But a relationship partnered with prayer is even more powerful and we needed both. When Luther and I thought we were expecting too much of others, we looked to scripture and Christ's example for our answers. Jesus had a deep spiritual connection with the Father through prayer and loved deep interpersonal human relationships. When Lazarus died and Jesus experienced Martha's grief and then the grief of Mary and the others, He wept (John 11:35). He prayed (John 11:41-42). He healed (John 11:43-44). Later on, after His crucifixion and ascension, Christ sent us the Holy Spirit, our comforter so we could have that same compassion with others and Godly power to live compassionately (Acts 2:17). Scripture teaches us that we do not need to be afraid to befriend the broken. We have divine authority to speak into the lives of others, even if it's uncomfortable.

In the midst of our chaos, I went on a mission trip to Lebanon to provide teaching to other missionaries in 2018. On this trip, the Lord brought me new friends. I only knew one woman well and we were partnered with two other ladies I had never met. Throughout the trip, we shared life stories and I told them of Sarah's struggles. I didn't have to educate them on addictions because they were experts in relationships. They just prayed for me and loved me. We laughed and cried together. Ate and worshiped. It was such a relief not to have to explain anything. When we returned, they wanted to meet Sarah and they actually made it happen! They came over several times, had coffee with her, and prayed over her. She was so grateful for those precious times. After Sarah's death, they checked in on me by calling and texting or dropping off goodies on my porch. I learned so much from these beautiful ladies about how to receive their gift of all-encompassing love and, in turn, how to give it.

I cannot say enough about having a network of supportive relationships. Your network is probably one of the most vital survival tools in this battle because none of us knows whether our loved one will overcome or succumb to addiction. You will need your people throughout every stage—find your forever friends! I have them. I have some that are the best texting friends. They seem to know when to send the perfect message or song at the right time. Then there are the "partners in crime" who will drop everything and drive hours to find your child on the side of the road, even if you haven't talked to them in months. You always need the praying friends who won't ask questions but will just listen and pray when you call. Fun friends who will make you laugh 'cause there's nothing else left to do. Baking friends. Seriously. You NEED THEM.

"Just the facts, ma'am" friends are incredible too. You know, the ones you call and ask a bizarre question, they give you a factual response and then you just hang up? I love those friends! Or the friends who will take over your business when you bluntly call and say, "Sarah's dead. I need you." They plan a repast and all you have to do is show up. These are deep heart friends. We have been extraordinarily blessed with rich friendships that have quite literally kept us going. I repeat, find your forever friends.

Supportive Church Environment

A critical part of our support was finding a church that loves broken people. For the record and biblically, this should be every church. Life is so much better when you're not the only family in the congregation with obvious issues. Attend a church with an open altar where your cries can be joined with the heartache of others. Such a spiritual family has truly been a vital part of our healing.

When Sarah's addiction first came to light, we were attending a church that shied away from messy. I think they truly wanted to love broken people but didn't know how. Many of the youth that I had pastored told their parents that my daughter was using drugs. Not one of those parents came to me; instead they encouraged their children to love Sarah from a distance. When I learned of this, it hurt. I mean, really hurt. It also hurt Sarah. Her cry for help seemed to warrant no assistance from the body of Christ.

I Peter 1:15 calls us to be holy, and Sarah was most definitely struggling in that area. I could not address her behavior because I didn't know about it. Sarah's peers who did know were young and needed the assistance of spiritually wise adults to help them. Matthew 18:15-17 explains how to go to the person who is caught in sin and restore them gently. Sarah's peers were too young and did not know how to do that. They needed their parents to assist by including me. If their parents didn't know how to do it, then they needed to go to the church leaders. The results still may have been the same but we cannot separate our members from the body (Matthew 18:17) preventing Christ to work in and through each of us to bring about restoration. For my part, I'm certain I wasn't perfect throughout Sarah's journey, and I have since asked for forgiveness from the people I have knowingly hurt. We grieved leaving that church and the people we loved dearly. But we were a family with deep needs that could not be spiritually supported there.

In retrospect, I don't think anybody really knew what to do. Including us. However, as the body of Christ, we are without excuse. If we don't know how to respond to depression or addiction, we need to learn or find the proper resources. "We don't know" is simply unacceptable. Avoidance is a sure death sentence either to the life of a congregation or the affected individuals. To me, this is an important area where we all can learn to take a good personal inventory of situations and our responses, without blame or shame. Examining our attitudes and actions may be uncomfortable but it allows us, both corporately and individually, to own what is our responsibility and move forward as kinder and more loving humans.

Family

My extended family has been absolutely stellar. Having limited knowledge of addictions or recovery, we all learned together. They also knew NOT to ask a lot of questions. It was exhausting and just sad to tell and retell stories. I learned that Sarah's actions brought her a lot of shame and embarrassment and it was not my job to perpetuate those feelings by repeating the gory details. My family respected that and Sarah needed her family outlet. She craved family. Even when she was horrible to her cousins or avoided her grandparents, she still craved their love and acceptance. By the grace of God, each family member loved Sarah deeply. Through laughter, letters, texts and tears our extended family was like a small love-mob. Subsequently, the grief we share from losing Sarah is intense.

One of the most precious gifts Sarah's grandmother gave her was a photo album to take with her wherever she was so that she would always know she was loved. Sarah took this album everywhere. Even in her darkest days she would hide it at the bottom of the totes she lived out of; it was always with her. Our family was determined to love Sarah regardless of situation or sobriety. We had to seek to find Sarah's love language and serve her there. Funny cards, Bible studies, journals and gift cards always followed Sarah to her next address. Blessings upon blessings for a daughter, granddaughter, niece and cousin whose addiction made her feel the sting of separation.

Forgiveness

Once we learned of Sarah's addiction, the loss of our privacy and identity happened rapidly. Who were we? This monster of addiction invaded our home and made our private lives very public. Drug dealers showed up at our door at all hours. Her fellow users came in like Eddie Haskell, "Hi Mrs. R," always spinning some new lie. (That's a "Leave it to Beaver" reference; I'm old). Can this be the house where all the youth group kids from church hung out and some even lived? We were caught in the emotional fray of trying to maintain a sense of normalcy and trying to find help for Sarah. Ultimately, we chose Sarah.

With this choice came many dishonorable behaviors we had to navigate. Stealing was probably the biggest. Drugs cost money and addicted individuals don't make good employees, so Sarah became quite an accomplished thief. At first it was cash. Small amounts because we didn't keep cash around. When Sarah was around I had to keep my purse hidden or attached to me. The loss of freedom in my own home angered and stung deeply. Or maybe it was the lying that followed? "How could you think I would ever steal from you?" she'd say, complete with crocodile tears. "I told you I would never do that! We will never have a relationship if you're always accusing me of stealing!" The emotional bondage of those moments repeatedly tested my sanity. Did I misplace my money? How much did I have in my purse anyhow? I was always rehashing these situations in my mind. I never wanted to falsely accuse Sarah because I knew how fragile she was.

After we learned not to keep *any* cash around, including change, the stealing got worse. She pawned my jewelry. I didn't own much jewelry of value so that stage ended very quickly, yet the hurt lasted the longest. Any nice earrings, rings and necklaces were gone. Each had had sentimental value—like my Sweet 16 ring and special original pieces purchased on my husband's travels. I was heartbroken.

It took me several years and many arguments with Sarah to heal from the thievery and lying. My privacy had been invaded and I felt violated. For me it wasn't "just jewelry." In an effort to keep my remaining jewelry and purses or clothes safe, we put locks on our bedroom door. My resentment smoldered. "Why do I have to suffer because you're addicted?" rolled through my mind on repeat. In my heart I knew that holding on to this bit-terness was not healthy and I asked the Lord to take the hatred and resent-ment towards Sarah from my heart. It didn't budge. I'd hear a small, still whisper in my mind, "Lay it down." I'd yell back, "I'm trying..."

The next few years passed with Sarah repeatedly and sincerely apolo-gizing for stealing my gems and lying about it. While she couldn't remain clean, we continued to work really hard on our relationship. I genuinely thought I'd forgiven her. Then one day we got into a deep discussion and she quietly said, "When will I be worth more to you than your jewelry?"

"What?" I said. "I'm really over that."

"No, Mom, you're not." And she proceeded to give me several valid examples of things I said or did that proved my lack of forgiveness. Ashamed, I looked at Sarah's tear-stained face and saw her anguish. I knew in that moment that I needed to truly forgive her and choose our relationship over my lost jewelry.

"I am so sorry," I said. "You will always be more precious to me than any of those jewels." And at that very moment, I was freed. To this day the bondage of my lost gems has no power over me. Thank you, Lord, for using Sarah to free ME!

Loving Boundaries

The inability to live without restrictions in our home was a big adjustment for all of us. We could no longer allow Sarah or her friends to come and go freely in our house, and she no longer had the privilege to call our house home. The pain was palpable for all of us. We wanted to be with each other uninhibited but addiction stole that from us.

When she was homeless and came to shower, she was only allowed in the first-floor bathroom. The door had to stay open with me standing guard outside. She was never allowed upstairs without an escort. Purses and backpacks were checked before coming into the house and leaving. Car keys were not left out. There were many times we would let our guard down only to hear one of our cars pull out of the yard, Sarah driving. Addiction didn't respect our relationship and so we learned it was our job to keep our boundaries. She wouldn't. She couldn't. It was no use blaming her. If we wanted peace in our home, it was up to us to establish and maintain it.

Living Grief

Family gatherings were another great loss. Because Sarah was loving, witty and smart, she added a dimension to our family functions that was dynamic. There were times she was too high to attend, and we all suffered because of her absence. Luther and I would smile bravely even though we missed her deeply. There were so many holidays spent in rehabs or birthdays celebrated in jail, yet we learned to make the best of it, even if it was just a 30-second phone call. We were always thankful for any connection.

There are such beautiful and helpful books on grief and loss. As of this writing, a favorite is "The Unwanted Gift of Grief: A Ministry Approach" by Tim P. VanDuivendyk, DMin. It is a powerful book that speaks to the grieving and those who serve them in ministry. I am having a love/hate relationship with its content as I work through it. It is comforting to be reminded that through the pain and loss, I am still so loved by the Father and that joy and sorrow can coexist. It blows my mind. I believe that someday all of my mourning will somehow turn to dancing, just as the Lord promises.

While our grief and loss are still very present, we continue to work through each day and each aspect of grief as it arises. Some weeks or months are so oddly normal and then a wave of sorrow rolls in to toss us around until we can find our footing once again. I began this book in December 2020, five months after Sarah died and thought it would be finished soon thereafter. Maybe I am a slow learner, but grief really didn't seem that bad in the first six months. Then, seemingly out of nowhere, pounding grief slammed into my heart and stopped the writing process for almost a year. I needed the constant badgering of my accountability partners to ask me with annoying frequency how the book was coming along. I tried to convince myself that the exercise of writing this book was not what Sarah and I had originally planned, but that it was for my own personal healing. That worked for a while. Then my friends would ask again, "Where's the book?" Groan.

I had to slowly examine why I couldn't finish this darn book. I prayed and wrote in my journal and wrestled with this question over and over in my mind. The honest answer was, I was scared. What if I couldn't remember the scriptures I used? What if people asked me questions I couldn't answer? And then, after all the years of saying, "I don't know," to my growing daughter's hard questions, that response now seemed so dumb. I decided I would not write another word until the Lord made it clear when and if I was to proceed. Remember Balaam's donkey (Numbers 22:21-39)? Yep, I had a donkey coming my way.

In December of 2021, Luther and I bought tickets for the musical "Hamilton." I had already seen it but he really wanted to go. As the date approached, I decided that I didn't want to go and offered my ticket to a family member who hadn't seen it. On the day of the musical, we found that a COVID-19 vaccination was required, ruling my family member out. So I reluctantly went. As the musical began, I was reminded of how much I loved it. The cast was different from my first viewing but still phenomenal. The actor that played Aaron Burr, Jr., however, annoyed me. He was extremely talented, but I just didn't like him. Every time he sang I just wanted to shoo him off the stage. During intermission, I asked Luther what he thought of the actor and he responded, "He's great." What the heck was the matter with me?

The musical proceeded and I forced myself to focus on the parts I loved. Then came the second-to-last song, "The World Was Wide Enough." In the song, Aaron Burr, Jr. abdicates responsibility for murdering Hamilton declaring that he was the one who ultimately suffered only to realize that indeed, the world had been wide enough for both of them.

As he continued to sing, it hit me like a freight train. This actor had the build, demeanor, and voice of the man that we believe gave Sarah her last hit of crack cocaine, delayed the call to 911 and ineffectively gave her CPR.

The day before she died, I insisted that we FaceTime. It was clear to me as she fidgeted that she was actively using. I asked her if she wanted help and she said no. The next day, July 13, 2020, we talked and texted most of the morning and into the afternoon and Sarah admitted how depressed she had become. I gave her my usual thousand-plus encouraging statements and she texted, "You may get discouraged but does it ever make you want to stick a needle in your arm and die?" My stomach heaved. She was in trouble. We text-prayed and she thanked me. Several hours later I checked in and there was no response. Three hours later I would get a call that Sarah had overdosed and died.

All of this is flashing through my mind as Aaron Burr, Jr. continues on with his bloody song. Uninvited tears popped from my eyes. Oh my goodness, the song is ending. Sandi, get it together. Stop crying! Lord, help me! I could feel myself slowly regaining a little self-control. Whew, thank you, Lord.

Then the last song began. The finale of all finales. Eliza Hamilton sings, "Who Lives, Who Dies, Who Tells Your Story." Are you kidding me?? As the character sang, each line pierced my heart, stealing my breath and striking painful blow after blow. Eliza had disappeared and I could see my Sarah urging me to tell our story. My tears flowed uncontrollably and I argued with the Lord, "No! I can't! Please. Not me..."

At this point, I knew the lights would be up at any second and I frantically tried to stop crying. The show ended and I kept my swollen eyes shut and my head down as we left the theater. My hero, Luther, who had no idea what was going on, pulled me through a sea of people. I received odd looks and stares. Faster, Luther. Please go faster. We finally made it outside and the bitter cold wind of Lake Erie lashed at my face. Finally, an excuse for tears. By the time we got into our car, I completely fell apart, sobbing and wailing (side note: I am quite certain the car next to us thought we were embroiled in an argument and stayed next to us a loooooong time). After what seemed like an eternity of sobbing, I finally asked my husband to leave before the police came. I sobbed relentlessly until I was finally able to tell Luther what had happened. He was so loving and patient. And I sobbed some more. Finally, I surrendered. Yes, Lord, I will write the book. Thank you, Lin-Manuel Miranda.

That moment of epiphany notwithstanding, we continue to grieve the loss of our daughter but the reality is that her losses were far greater than ours. She lost many beautiful friends to addiction. All of them she loved greatly. All of them we came to love, too. So many funerals, apologies and tears. Epic proportions of grief and loss confused her heart and lied to her spirit. The shame and sorrow were so profound she often lost the ability to function. We watched the walls grow thicker and her survival skills dwindle. Praying always for the truth to set her free.

Scriptures for Consideration

Hebrews 12:1-2 (NKJV) *"Therefore we also, since we are surrounded by so great a cloud of witnesses, let us lay aside every weight, and the sin which so easily ensnares us, and let us run with endurance the race that is set before us, looking unto Jesus, the author and finisher of our faith, who for the joy that was set before Him endured the cross, despising the shame, and has sat down at the right hand of the throne of God." (Sarah's choice)*

I John 1:9 (NASB) *"If we confess our sins, He is faithful and righteous to forgive us our sins and to cleanse us from all unrighteousness."*

Matthew 18:21-22 (ESV) *"Then Peter came to Jesus and said, 'Lord, how many times will my brother sin against me and I forgive him, up to seven times?' Jesus said to him, 'I tell you, not seven times but seventy times seven!'"*

Mark 11:25 (GNT) *"And when you stand and pray, forgive anything you may have against anyone, so that your Father in heaven will forgive the wrongs you have done."*

Psalm 147:3 (NLT) *"He heals the broken-hearted and bandages their wounds."*

Psalm 73:26 (NIV) *"My flesh and my heart may fail, but God is the strength of my heart and my portion forever."*

2 Corinthians 4:8-9 (KJV) *"We are troubled on every side, yet not distressed, we are perplexed, but not in despair; persecuted, but not forsaken; cast down but not destroyed."*

Music to Inspire

"Goodness of God," Jenn Johnson
"Forgiven," Sanctus Real
"I'd Do It Again (Live)," Tasha Cobbs
"Forgiveness," TobyMac (featuring Lecrae)
"You Reign," William Murphy

Chapter 9

Relapse

"Now the Lord is the Spirit, and where the
Spirit of the Lord is, there is freedom."
2 Corinthians 3:17 (NIV)

(No date)

Just for Today:
Find something positive about yourself. Get deep; self
reflect and know that the feelings and sadness aren't permanent. As cliche as it is, feelings aren't facts, and just for today,
you're alive and ok.

June 26, 2013

*Always ask questions.
Remember to pray for:
-understanding

-peace and serenity
-help in general
-self esteem issues.
God grant me the serenity to accept the things I cannot change, courage to change the things I can and the wisdom to know the difference.

June 27, 2013

Saw my mom today!! Kinda by accident but a blessing in disguise nonetheless! GRATITUDE!!! She started to cry. But for the first time in a while, tears of happiness! Weeeeeeeee! Anyways, off to bed I go. I hope tomorrow proves to be a better day!
Prayers:
-wisdom to know the difference
-discernment
-good judgement

July 12, 2013

"I dig my toes into the sand,
The ocean looks like a thousand diamonds
Strewn across a blue blanket:
I lean into the wind
Pretending that I am weightless,
And in this moment I am
HAPPY; HAPPY."

June 10, 2019

I'm so empty and lost and confused again. It's been I think 3 weeks since I left Levittown and I am back at negative square one. I should've just stayed and finished the darn program. Why couldn't I just give myself that extra couple of weeks to heal?? WHAT IS WRONG WITH ME!?! I'm so disappointed in myself. I'm so sad. I don't know what to do. Now I have backed myself into a freakin' corner AGAIN except this time I can't just be like ok "I should go back to detox." Nope, because I'm in supportive living and would not have anywhere to go afterwards.

I was fine. I thought I was fine and strong in my recovery coming home from there. As in I felt different...much more different than I ever have before. I had a great plan in place and people ready and willing to help me at every obstacle. 25 minutes from Buffalo on the car ride home, I had the most intense craving to compromise my recovery. It's like, I skipped the entire emotional relapse piece and just went straight for it. How did that even happen??? I'm racking my brain trying to figure out what led me here? Did it start long before I actually picked up? I didn't think so. I tried to humble myself as best I could. I wasn't acting out on any addictive behaviors AND I was talking about it. Talking about everything that has previously led me to relapse and how I could prevent it this time!!!! I believe I was being receptive to feedback and implementing suggestions the best I could.

Dammit Dammit Dammit why couldn't I just stay and finish that f-ing program!!!! No, it wasn't a helpful program but F*** I would've at least come out of that joint with two months of clean time and a daily routine. Dammit Sarah what in the F*** is wrong with you!!!!

Lord, I feel so beyond hopeless. I don't think another treatment is going to be the answer but then what.... God, I honestly thought and felt like I was 100% done this time. I felt different-more than I ever have in the past and apparently not. So, where do I even go from here? What do I even do differently My whole entire existence is either recovery or relapse and there is and will never be an in-between. I'm struggling to find the missing link?

I'm in a sober house with all these amazing women who are actually trying their darnedest to get this sh**...and here I am trying to play the system again-wasting time again for what? A place to live? I guess so. So I don't have to go back to treatment? I guess so. I can't even be honest with my sponsor. That's the worst part. Like she probably already knows something is up, and I can't even muster the courage to tell her of all people, the truth. Like WHY!! It's nothing off her back. I'm only wasting my time and hurting myself.

June 19, 2019

I don't know why I could never get this program but others could. It doesn't make sense. For the past few years, I wanted it way more than countless others. I tried my damndest and can never f-ing do it. I have felt so hopeless for the past few years and have prayed and prayed and can never ever maintain. I have so many blessings that I just sh** over and it's like I can't stop myself!

I am trying so hard to not be pitying but like, how the f*** Can I not? I have been trying and like I can never meet my own or anyone else's expectations-and it's killing me!

June 27, 2019

Three days until July 1st. Three days until rent's due. I have three days to decide WTF do I do? WTF am I even doing?

I can't stop God!! Do I seriously have to go to detox and rehab again just to put the stuff down? Am I that bad/ obsessed? I'm semi hopeful about the subs, but what if I can't even get 24 hours without doing dope so I can start it?? I am so trapped, Lord. I feel completely unwanted at this house and I honestly don't even blame them. I wouldn't want to live with someone I'm 85% sure is using either. I wouldn't want to live with someone who seems like they are just using this house as a flop house either!! To the outsider it probably seems like I would give a flying F about recovery. Like I just want to be sneaky and do me.

I wish anyone would believe me if I told them that this isn't the case at all. That I'm dying inside but I have no idea what to do and am too scared of being honest that I've been using every single day since I moved in. That I'm dying to stop and be free like the other girls. That I'm dying to join in their antics and be a part of but my disease is keeping me iso- lated and lonely. That I wake up every morning hoping that this will be the day that I won't use and that every night I put my head on the pillow as a failure.

I'm so sick of being a liar and covering for my disease. Why is it so hard for me to be thoroughly honest??? It's like I lie to the bitter end to the point where everyone is sick of the words that come out of my mouth and to the point where I am completely humiliated because I let it go on for so long.

July 7, 2019

I've got to start my subs [suboxone] tomorrow. How is it that I can't get through 1 day without using?? Even using I'm unsatisfied so much, except the first 20 seconds-so now that is what I live for-the first 20 seconds after taking a shot.

Once again, I got nothing I needed to get done, done today like an effing moron. I'm trying to trust God but I really need this obsession removed from me! Please God take away the mental obsession. For long enough so I can start my subs and take care of the physical illness.

- Read out the 12/12 with my sponsor. Went to 1/1. Got a group schedule.
- Mom's house.
- 5 or 7 pm meeting

July 12, 2019

Got out of jail today. I can't believe it but then again I sorta can. Of course I f-n used today. But-I got my car taken. It occurred to me that I walked miles to get 2 bags. By the time I got home I was exhausted, not high and out $20. I realized that I do not and will not go to those lengths for my drug anymore. Not anymore. I just can't.

I'm blessed that I can still live here.

July 28, 2019

I didn't have to use today. I stole money from mom and did anyways. Ugh. Hopefully tomorrow will be a success. I don't understand how [name] and [name] can do it, even [name] can do it. I'm so annoyed with myself. I just want to move on and move forward from this like so bad. I want to be successful at things in my life and do things I enjoy. I can feel it-I'm almost there and then the devil is just pushing harder than ever. Man, God I trust You. I'm so stuck in this b/s routine that I feel so angry when I can't fulfill it-even though I want to be clean more than anything. It's the first week I have to push through and the devil is holding me down.

God help me draw near to you so I can resist the devil in my mind. Lord take the lies and excuses from my lips and let me hold fast to the truth.

Teach me Father to walk and talk like your Son! I want to broaden and get more intimate in our relationship, Lord. I want to know You deeply and spread that love.

July 30, 2019

Reading today's devo made me think! It was all about Shadrach, Meshach, Abednego, and Nebuchadnezzar. Sometimes I forget that the God that literally made them free is the same God in our world today on July 30th. It's so weird just because I don't ever see miracles like that happening, like big certifiably impossible miracles. Somehow God's power has been limited over time or got lazy or something. Lord please open my eyes to see your miracles today. Soften my heart to be appreciative to Your small yet still magnificent miracles happening everyday all around. Move me to cleanse and take care of Your temple and most of all cleanse me of my doubt Father. Help me to comprehend that you're the same yesterday, today and tomorrow. Amen.

July 31, 2019

Last day of July. I shouldn't have used but I did. My dose is getting up to where I can't really feel it, which is technically great but will be something to grieve probably.

Goal for today; start doing some digging. Lord I ask you to reveal to me what issue(s) I need to really be focusing on deep, deep down as to why I use and am constantly trying to ruin your temple.

Open my eyes God as to how I am to step into my purpose. Or more honestly, how not to use for tomorrow. Thank you for the path you've set before me. Thy will be done. Amen.

August 26, 2019

Wow, I haven't journaled for a whole month. Maybe almost two. How does time go so fast when I'm using yet so slow when I try and do right?

I think I'm going to go into detox tomorrow. I can't keep putting it off. This has gone on long enough and I obviously can't kick the dope on my own. I keep trying and trying. It's been like four months of "I'll stay clean tomorrow" and I think I've been off dope for 2 single days in the past months.

I don't even get high and so as soon as the rush fades I feel so empty and desolate-yet I can't stop.

Halfheartedly asking for help-Where's the other half? Where did it go? Is it there? Am I not looking hard enough or is it that I'm not looking at all?

Begs for forgiveness; feeling the reapers dank breath on my neck. I'm sorry God. Will this be it? Please I'll get it right...tomorrow...full measures...tomorrow.

Where is today? How do I do today? Hundreds of todays-now baby is 25, hardly alive, hands to the sky, begging HOW?? WTF??

What will it add up to? Unfulfilled potential she couldn't pick up a pencil, to know the stranger that mechanically moves for her.

Dying to be heard, known.

Knocks, the door cracks, she peeks uncertain of the I AM behind the curtain-It's a lie-constantly hides behind the lies she tells herself.

You can come in tomorrow.

September 4, 2019

$500 gone in a day. $50 worth of food stamps to last me 30 days. I'm so sick of myself. I'm sick of my life and all of the characters in it. Two days out of detox. God I can't take this!! Help me with the desperation and motivation to help myself Lord. I'm dying. I'm so hurt and broken and troubled inside God. I don't want success and all that, I just want peace. Your peace. It doesn't seem to matter what verses I read, pray, go to meetings. I still wake up daily and make the choice to use. I need help so badly. I can't stand the sight of myself, my skin, my own thoughts even are driving me nuts. Lord how do I let You take the wheel?

October 10, 2019

...I wonder if all of our family and friends who have come into Speak Easy who have said how wonderful I look...I wonder if they can see how empty I am. I wonder or if they are just fishing for something, anything to say to me. I'm quickly losing my ability to connect with others. It's scaring me. I forget what regulars talk about. What are interests and hobbies?

I am ice cold/barely there to mom and Luth and so sorry for that. I wish so badly to be present with them for they are the ones I cherish the most. I didn't use the word "love" because the way I act towards them of late is not that of love and I believe "love" to be an action word, and not to be thrown around loosely. I want my soul. Not ¼ of it. Not some of it. I want my full soul to reach out and touch the Spirit of Christ and of others. I want contentment. I plead with death to let me get there first. I'm also having questions of my salvation. I believe with everything in me-but I am deliberately disobeying Him in the name of addiction.—I don't want to say I can't help it, but as my insides cry out in agony, my body just goes. It's a shame that the only times I'm ever able to stop is when I'm locked away. It's sad and unfortunate and I wish that were not the case. I wish I just "wanted it" bad enough to say enough is enough.

Oh, but I do.

October 19, 2019

Day 1 back at Total Freedom. I swear to God I can't believe I'm back here. I know deep down it is what I need-YOU are what I need Lord-but holy crap I don't know if I'm ready God. Completely done...I don't know.... Lord, why is it so hard to give up the flesh? I pray my heart will be opened and my mind also.

October 20, 2019

I'm so uncomfortable. It's only morning still-but I'm having an awful lot of doubts. I have so much healing to do. It all seems like a lot right now. Remember to take it piece by piece-a day at a time and try not to freak out about things that haven't even happened yet. Today is today and that's all there is for right now. So chill the F*** out.

March 7, 2020

Sarah,

Heard you were having an off day. It's ok. That's life some-times and just because you get sober doesn't mean that life stops or respects that.

1. *Take a step back and breathe.*
2. *Call or talk to someone in recovery and use specific emotions.*
3. *Try and get a meeting and if that's not an option do anything to be around others. You know how your mind festers.*
4. *Maybe call your cousin Sam-you know you always laugh together.*

Just keep in mind before your wheels start turning that feelings don't last forever and this will pass.

Xo Sarah
Songs:
"Killa Cam"-Camron
"Melodies from Heaven"-Kirk Franklin
"Clarinet Concerto No 1"-Mozart

January 4, 2020

> -Work on praying, genuinely
> -Dialogue throughout the day
> -Be more mindful of what I'm doing when it's just me
>   and God
> -Serenity Prayer
> -Put action behind prayers
> -Watch how I talk to myself
> -Seek what makes me genuinely feel close to God

March 2020

> Philosophies of Life
> Sarah—
>
> How do you picture yourself tomorrow? Next week? Next year?
>
> Do your words reflect your actions?
>
> How are you treating others? Hopefully with the same concern and compassion that you would want from somebody else.
>
> Are you an active participant in your own life and do you wake up with a sense of purpose?
>
> Are you honest with yourself and others and do you show up and keep your word?
>
> Ponder these questions as you go forward and strive for a greater meaning.

Understanding that relapse can be part of the recovery process was the hardest concept for me to grasp. It seemed that if people in recovery knew that relapse was an option, then one's mind, even subconsciously, would perseverate on using one more time. At least that's the way Sarah described it to me. As tortured as her entries read, she held onto her addiction as a resource. If all else failed, she still had drugs. Initially this made no sense to me, but as the years passed and sobriety eluded her, I began to understand her pained thinking. For some people, the concept of relapsing saved them from the despondency of chronic failure and enabled them to refocus on the success of their clean time. For Sarah, it was an open door that needed to be shut. She understood that but couldn't close it.

Although painful to admit it, Sarah was a classic self-sabotager. This was a pattern that started much earlier in life. When an activity became too uncomfortable for her, she would find a way to withdraw emotionally, physically or both. This was especially true in rehab. As the end of a 28-day program would draw near, the inevitable internal conflict would rage: Sarah's mind telling her that she was ready to go and her heart begging her to stay for deeper healing. The only program post-high school she ever completed was a job-training program intended for immigrants, yet, that little certificate meant the world to her. Unfortunately, Sarah was never able to translate that success into recovery.

Sometimes, our fear borne out of experience made Luther and me guilty of "aiding and abetting." Too many times, Sarah would complete the detox phase of a program and would start the next phase but be asked to leave immediately because she broke a rule (or twenty). This usually happened somewhere in a remote setting hours from our home, making Luther and I weigh the pros and cons of once again going to pick her up: if we left her on the side of the road to reap the consequences of her actions, would we be able to find her if something bad happened or do we bring her home and allow her to work out the details with the staff of drug court? The latter always seemed safer. However, as we watched this cycle repeat itself over time, we knew her future was completely out of our hands.

Relapse wasn't just a concept we bristled against. It scared us. When Sarah would relapse she almost always overdosed, requiring Narcan© or other life-saving measures. Her mind would tell her to use the same amount she used last time, but her drug-free body was no longer able to tolerate such large doses and would result in an overdose. Because of this, we kept Narcan© kits everywhere in our house, garage and cars. It only took once for me to see Sarah's blue body and hear the death gurgle coming from her lungs to get trained and remain prepared. We needed to do what we could, while we could.

After one relapse and overdose, Sarah came home from the hospital shaken. She stayed very close to us for days. When we asked her what was wrong, she told us that during her overdose she could feel herself falling down deeper and deeper into a black hole. She screamed for Jesus. Right before she fell through the final dark doors, Sarah felt herself being grabbed and drawn into the light. This confirmed her understanding of heaven and hell, which she knew to be real places. The memory of this experience scared her so much that she insisted on being baptized. She remained clean for her longest time after this near-death encounter. Sadly and slowly, her eyes left Jesus and she resumed her repeated cycle of overdose and recovery.

During Sarah's second last relapse we were forced to acknowledge that we couldn't change the outcome of her cycles. We made the difficult decision—once again—to let her live the way she chose regardless of the outcome. Sarah could no longer hide her use and refused assistance. She felt hopeless to try again. After disappearing for a few days, Sarah texted and said she needed help. I prayed for her to find a solution as I was determined that I would no longer intervene. On the third night, after having gone to bed, I had this urge to search for programs designed for those who chronically relapse. I found a program in Florida that used music in recovery. I took a screenshot and sent it to her. Hours later, Sarah sent a text saying she would give it a try. We had just one rule: regardless if she finished the program, Sarah could not come home for one year. She agreed and the next morning she made the phone call and was accepted. I had an hour to pack her bags, find her and get her to the airport. When I picked her up, Sarah was a mess, at the end of a high and the beginning of withdrawal, pale and shaking. I got her into the airport, checked her luggage and sent her through security but by then she had used up any energy she had and was standing still, staring off into space. She only had five minutes to get to the gate and needed to move quickly. I caught a security guard's attention and asked for assistance in getting Sarah to the gate. He looked at me, looked at her and kindly guided her to the plane.

The first phase of the program was wonderful. Her counselor challenged her at every opportunity. She responded well and actually enjoyed the painful process of getting to know herself again. Her attitude was different from her previous attempts at sobriety. Soon Sarah was moved to the next stage of the program and was given a new counselor. They were a mismatch with the counselor weekly asking ME how to reach my daughter. Sarah became discouraged and requested a new counselor to no avail. I began to worry that old habits would re-emerge. To complicate matters, it was March 2020 and the COVID-19 pandemic necessitated that regular programming be conducted remotely. Little else was done to inspire and encourage the residents.

Sarah was disappointed that there was nothing and no one to challenge her. Soon old habits of sleeping all day and flirting with opportunistic relationships began. She recognized what was happening yet couldn't stop herself. Ingrained patterns of behavior were superseding any newly acquired healthy lifestyle choices. Thankfully, as the inevitable decline was setting in, Sarah got a job and her self-confidence slowly returned. Against all odds, her hope was at an all-time high.

This job had long hours and she was good at it. Not a dream job, but a professional job and despite COVID, still working in-person at a nice office with equally nice co-workers. We talked about making friends and how awkward she felt. We discussed transportation and ways to keep actively involved in recovery.

Within a few weeks of working, Sarah, along with several people from her sober living complex decided to move in together. We encouraged her to remain in sober living but the combined excitement of a new job, a newly positive outlook and the lack of extensive COVID regulations was more inviting. She also began dating a young man who took recovery seriously and challenged Sarah to communicate effectively. What a difference we began to hear in her voice! Somewhat miraculously, she even talked about learning how to budget.

Despite all the positive things happening in her life, Sarah was homesick. She was missing me and I her, so I took a COVID risk and traveled down to see her. What a blessing that trip was. We had such tender moments. Because she was working, we only had evenings, but made the best of every moment. We laughed. Walked the beach. Held hands.

Leaving Florida, the new living situation still didn't feel right to me. Everyone was too new in recovery to properly support each other. It was too risky for them all and we saw a slow decline in Sarah's positive outlook. Luther and I prayed for her and with her. We encouraged her to participate in online recovery meetings, talk to her cousins or call us. She would call regularly and say, "I know I can't come home but can you talk me through this…?" And we would.

Within a month at her new job, she was offered training for a promotion. This was unheard of for any employee under six months at the company. Sarah was so proud of herself. Two weeks later, all employees were sent home to work remotely. Not good! Sarah and isolation equaled a death sentence. In the beginning, she put her learning to practice and called me throughout her workday to show me she was outside getting fresh air or with her roommates. Sarah knew herself well enough to know she needed accountability.

It was an upswing that did not last. At some point after Sarah began working from home, a roommate relapsed. She was not far behind. Her calls went from daily to a text every other day to every couple of days. I knew that pattern well. Luther and I pondered the obvious implications and jointly agreed to let Sarah take any next steps. She had the tools and knew the way forward if she wanted to take it; there was not anything more we could do for her. I received calls from a program support person multiple times reporting that Sarah was not returning calls and was rumored to be using again. There was no intervention offered. I was 1300 miles away and Sarah was an adult. Frustrated, I prayed. Still, there was a peace in my heart to let her be. So I did.

A roommate moved out and a new roommate—a rumored drug dealer—moved in. "Are you sure you want this guy in the house?" we asked Sarah.

"Yes, Mom."

On Sunday, July 12, after several days of silence, I called via FaceTime, knowing she'd most likely pick up for our Sunday night call. Sarah did, keeping herself hidden in the dark but I encouraged her to show us her beautiful face. She moved to a semi-lit room and Luther and I had our confirmation. The dark circles and pick marks on her face were back. Her legs were twitching and she couldn't sit still. We talked and I encouraged Sarah to reach out to her sponsor or close friends in recovery. She said she was depressed but not using. Sigh. We told each other how much we loved each other and hung up. Sarah promised to start calling every day again.

As you now know, the next day she overdosed and died. I fumbled around after I received the news. As I prepared to tell my husband, I heard this faint yet audible voice in my head say, "I'm sorry." I sat very still for a few tearful moments as I do not believe that the dead talk. What I think people hear is the enemy choosing to use the voices of the dead to divert people from truth or the Truth Giver. But this was not Sarah's voice. As I sat weeping, I knew the Holy Spirit was with me and I was profoundly grateful. I knew Sarah was with the Father. God is good even in the darkest hour. He knew my daughter well and had planned her rescue. His tender mercies are new every morning. Great is His faithfulness.

The Aftermath

The police called and we were introduced to a compassionate detective who helped us through the next steps and who would continue to be our contact for several months. During our initial conversation we learned that his wife grew up 15 minutes from our home and her parents still live here. We chatted about our favorite stores and restaurants. Thank you, Lord, for knitting these small comforting details into this horrific day. We made arrangements to fly down the next day, as we were not really sure what would be done with Sarah's body. Do we identify her? How long does it take to do an autopsy? Would we be able to see her before she was cremated? So many dark, random questions.

As we walked through the airport to the gate, I involuntarily slowed to a stop; my legs would not let me move. I just couldn't do this. My husband patiently waited until my mind allowed my body to move again. Finally on the plane, I thought I would lose my mind, the thoughts of all we had to do were surreal and overwhelming. My go-to worship music didn't help. Reading was not an option. Lord, I'm going to freak out, please keep my mind at ease. As I closed my eyes and tried to rest, Woody from Toy Story popped in my head, singing rather loudly, "You've Got a Friend In Me." "Really, Lord? I'm going to have Randy Newman echoing in my head?" Yup, for the entire flight. "Thank you, Father. You know all my needs." So, with a little smile on my face, and Randy Newman in my ears, I endured the most painful flight of my life.

Once settled in our hotel, the phone calls started. Find a funeral home. Call the morgue. Get the police report. Contact Sarah's roommate to get her belongings. At some point, it all just became a blur. I couldn't make sound decisions. "Lord, I need you to clear my head!!!" "The good work I began in you, I will bring to completion" came to my mind. (Philippians 1:6 paraphrased). I repeated this over and over in my head until all the details were taken care of. My husband was my earthly caretaker and my heavenly Father took care of my mental and spiritual details. Everything I needed for that torturous day was lovingly provided.

That same day, we made arrangements with the new roommate to pick up Sarah's belongings. I felt in my heart that this roommate was the person who was supplying Sarah with drugs. My husband and I prayed before we went and asked the Lord for a special measure of grace. We met this young man at the door and he insisted on hugging me, leaving me no option to refuse. I'm not exactly sure how I did it, but I hugged him back. As Luther watched this extension of unwanted affection, he expressed the most incredible amount of self-control imaginable. We just wanted to get her things. The young man just wanted to walk us through the scenario of her overdose, his life saving attempts, what she looked like and where she was lying. The whole story, from beginning to end.

Somewhere along the way, I felt sorry for this young man. He was so deep into either selling or using that he no longer responded to death with any emotion. It was all just so sad. Just like Sarah had to live with the con-sequences of using with other people that overdosed or died, he would have to do the same. "The enemy comes only to steal, kill and destroy..." John 10:10

We excused ourselves and went to collect her belongings. "Lord, please let us keep moving." Ultimately, the paramedics and police found no drug paraphernalia anywhere in the three-story condominium or on or near Sarah's body—an impossibility without human intervention. The police badly wanted an arrest, but there was no evidence.

It took the county coroner several days to release Sarah's body to the funeral home due to the record number of COVID-19 and overdose deaths. We decided upon cremation and at the funeral home, we didn't find an urn we liked so we set out to find the perfect container in which to bring her home. We mindlessly wandered through stores looking for anything cre-ative that would hold her ashes. Nothing. On our way out of the last store, we looked over at the handbags. Sarah loved a good handbag. I thought, why couldn't we put her ashes in a purse? Was it sacrilegious? A purse for an urn? Nope, it was just the right thing. We found a pink Michael Kors purse on clearance. Sarah would have loved that. Classy *and* cheap! So we bought the bag we affectionately nicknamed the "purn."

In the days to follow, the Lord provided emotional distractions for us, usually humorous, no matter where we went. Still in Florida, we just wanted to find a peaceful place where there was no noise. We found the most isolated section of the beach and bam, girls gone wild plop next to us! We moved to another spot and bam, families gone wild. AHHHHHH! Help us, Lord.

Before we left Florida, we were able to see Sarah's body before it was to be cremated. As difficult as it was to see my beautiful girl lifeless, there was some small, odd comfort in seeing the signs of regular use rather than a single relapse. Her once luxurious hair, limp and dull. Her face with pick marks, the evidence of repeated use. We kissed her goodbye and made our way out. Sarah was no longer there. She was home with the Father.

As we gathered our things to leave the funeral parlor, we were informed that there was one last piece of paper to sign: a waiver that said that if the postal service loses her remains, the funeral home was not responsible. I laughed and said, "Sarah wouldn't mind that. It would be her last great adventure." The woman just stared at me; she didn't seem to share my morbid sense of humor. I'm certain Sarah was laughing.

We returned home and held a memorial service amid the love of friends and family. To our surprise the church was filled with a diverse, eclectic gathering of people who had known Sarah over the years. She touched many during her short life. And so now we learn to live, one day at a time, without a call, text or visit—all of our future celebrations to be endured without her. We live expectantly knowing that one day we will see her whole and perfect in heaven. We will enjoy eternity together there, forever praising and worshipping and relapse will never be an issue.

Scriptures for Consideration

Galatians 5:13 (ESV) *"For you were called to freedom, brothers. Only do not use your freedom as an opportunity for the flesh, but through love serve one another."*

2 Corinthians 3:17 (NIV) *"Now the Lord is the Spirit, and where the Spirit of the Lord is, there is freedom."*

John 8:32 (ESV) *"And you will know the truth and the truth will set you free."*

Psalm 118:5 (ESV) *"Out of my distress I called on the Lord; the Lord answered me and set me free."*

Romans 8:2 (ESV) *"For the law of the Spirit of life has set you free in Christ Jesus from the law of sin and death."*

I Corinthians 9:19 (ESV) *"For though I am free from all, I have made myself a servant to all, that I might win more of them."*

Revelation 21:4 (ESV) *"He will wipe away every tear from their eyes, and death shall be no more, neither shall there be mourning, nor crying, nor pain anymore, for the former things have passed away."*

Music to Inspire

"Don't Give Up," Kirk Franklin, Hezekiah Walker, Donald Lawrence, Karen Clark
"No Longer Slaves," Jonathan David, Melissa Helsa
"21 Years," Toby Mac
"Freedom," Jesus Culture
"Freedom," Eddie James
"Ain't No Grave," Bethel Music & Molly Skaggs

Chapter 10

Where Do We Go From Here?

> *"Humble yourself in the sight of the*
> *Lord, and He will lift you up."*
> Hebrews 4:10 (NKJ)

March 2020 (To the tune of "Dancing Queen" by Abba)

> *You can dance*
> *You're alive*
> *Having the strength to survive*
> *See that girl*
> *Watch that scene*
> *Digging the Dope-less Queen*

(No Date)

> *Dear Addiction,*
> *Bye.*
> *Sarah*

I hope as you complete this book, you are changing. I know I am. Does your heart cry out more for those who are lost or in bondage? Mine does. Is your theology just a little bit messier and clearer at the same time? Mine is. The process of writing this book was painful and it made me seek the Lord more and differently. I had to re-examine many foundational scriptures. I had to come before the Lord with a new honesty. In return, He has given me peace. He has given me forgiveness and the freedom to forgive. He has given me a new song of praise. I'm not quite sure exactly how it sounds or whether it's even in tune, but it's rich and gritty.

I will never know why Jesus didn't deliver Sarah this side of Heaven. But oddly enough, the answer isn't very important to me anymore. What I do know is that God is Holy and everything He has planned for our lives is good. As believers we can experience His goodness daily. It may not feel good all the time, but that doesn't make His Word any less true. So, I cling to His promises instead of my emotions, knowing that someday, all of our suffering will have been for His glory. Today, that has to be enough.

I have also realized that our relationship with the Father, Son, and Holy Spirit is very intimate by design. We draw near to Him and He draws near to us. Each simple step brings us closer to the one true and living God who is waiting to lavish His love on us. Sarah, in her own way, took steps towards Him through her writings, prayer and worship. Today, she has the answers that she needed.

When I don't understand the work of His hands, I can trust His heart. He is good. He loves my daughter even more than I do. And there is no part of addiction that scares Him. There's no part of Sarah's torment that was ever too much for him.

My heart will always miss my woobie, Sarah Lou, but as I lay her story down, I can only pray it brings you life, eternal life. That would be her desire. Maybe somewhere you hear a young woman singing freely in Italian, filling the heavenlies with her song. A song of worship to the King of Kings. Her Healer. Her Savior. May you find Him as yours today.

Final Heart Scriptures

Hebrews 4:10 (NKJ) *"Humble yourself in the sight of the Lord, and He will lift you up."* (Sarah's choice)

I Peter 3:9 (NLT), *"The Lord isn't really being slow about his promise, as some people think. No, He is being patient for our sake. He does not want anyone to be destroyed, but wants everyone to repent."*

Romans 10:9 (NLT), *"If you openly declare that Jesus is Lord and believe in your heart that God raised Him from the dead, you will be saved."*

John 3:16-17 (NASB), *"For God so loved the world that He gave His only begotten Son, that whoever believes in Him shall not perish, but have eternal life. For God did not send the Son into the world to judge the world, but that the world might be saved through Him."*

Parting Songs

"Barocha," Michael Card (Sarah's favorite bedtime song since birth)
"For Those Tears I Died," Marsha Stevens-Pino

Resources

Addictions-A Banquet in the Grave: Finding Hope in the Power of the Gospel. Edward T. Welch shows how addictions result from a worship disorder-idolatry-and how they are overcome by the power of the gospel. 978-0-87552-606-5

Switch On Your Brain: The Key to Peak Happiness, Thinking, and Health. Dr. Caroline Leaf. Dr. Leaf teaches you the science and Scripture behind the amazing, God-given power we have within our minds. 978-0-8010-1830-8

50 Days Of Heaven: Reflections That Bring Eternity To Light. Randy Alcorn. Alcorn brings eternity to light in 50 inspiring and thought-provoking meditations that will forever change the way you think about the spectacular new universe that awaits us. 978-1-4143-0976-7

Through The Eyes Of A Lion: Facing Impossible Pain, Finding Incredible Power. Levi Lusko. Lusko teaches the reader how to face adversity or to prepare yourself for inevitable hardship through Jesus' eyes. 978-0-7180-3214-2

The Unwanted Gift Of Grief: A Ministry Approach. Tim P. VanDuiendyk, DMin. VanDuiendyk. VanDuiendyk offers direction to professionals working with people experiencing grief, individuals who are grieving and friends and family who walk closely with loved ones in grief. 978-0-7890-2950-8

Holier Than Thou: How God's Holiness Helps Us Trust Him. Jackie Hill Perry. Perry walks us through Scripture, shaking the dust off of "holy" as we've come to know it and revealing it for what it is: good news. She shows us how God isn't like us. He is holy. That's exactly what makes Him trustworthy. 978-1-5359-7571-1

Chapter 1: Questions to ponder

What or who can help you work through these pages? Sometimes reading painful stories can trigger negative thoughts. I encourage you to find a partner or a group that will help you to work through the tough spots.

Describe your family dynamics and their evolution.

Do you struggle with parts of your family's story? If so, which?

Have you ever invited the Lord into those places of struggle? What did that look like?

Has the Lord answered you? If so, how? (ex. I had incredible peace and contentment as a single mother)

Chapter 2: Questions to Ponder

How would you characterize your faith? (Active, discerning, developing, absent) Are you content with your faith?

When have you felt like Sarah; wanting so hard to please the Lord and yet not feeling like you ever can?

Who can you speak with to discuss concerns about your faith? Make a date with this person.

Sarah read the Bible, prayed and listened to podcasts. What can or do you do to draw closer to Christ?

Suggestions:

-Find a Bible-based pastor, friend, or counselor and seek out the answers to any of your faith questions; especially those regarding repentance, spiritual growth and blind faith.

-Practice talking to and listening to the Father. He is waiting. (Hint: Prayer is talking to the Lord and reading His word helps us "hear" Him.)

Chapter 3: Questions to Ponder

How do you see the Father, Son, and Holy Spirit working in your life?

How have you been able to trust God with your whole heart (in calm and crises)? If you can't, what's getting in the way?

Ask the Holy Spirit to reveal himself to you. His name is "Helper" and His purpose is to help you. Ask Him to help you draw near to the Lord and do His will. Write down any instances in which you have seen the evidence of the Holy Spirit working in your life.

Chapter 4: Questions to Ponder

To which part of this chapter can you relate? Why?

When have you, a family member or close friend ever felt depressed or suicidal?

Have you (or they) ever tried to self-treat the symptoms of depression? If so, how? Did it help?

Are you willing to talk to a health care professional about your symptoms? (Physician, counselor, recovery coach, etc)

Which people in your life can help find the proper resources to address your concerns?

Chapter 5: Questions to Ponder

Did Sarah's words shock you? How do you relate to them?

Do you know where you or the person you care about is in the addiction process?

Whether you are the person addicted or a family/friend, whom can you talk to?

What are your support networks?

Can you identify what may be holding you back from moving forward? (Fear, lack of knowledge, shame, another person's addiction...) Pray for the Lord to direct your next steps in regard to this list.

If your church has a recovery ministry, would you be willing to participate or volunteer? If your church doesn't have a ministry ask them to refer you to a nearby program.

Resources:

Alcoholics Anonymous: aa.org
Narcotics Anonymous: na.org
SAMHSA's National helpline: 800.622.4357
Dial 411 or Crisis Services in most areas in the USA

Chapter 6: Questions to Ponder

What values are important in your family? Honesty, respect, open communication...

Which strategies do you use to deal with difficult situations like addiction in your family?

What kind of support does your family offer when difficult situations arise?

What type of support do you or your family need?

Google search keywords like; support groups near me, family counselors near me, recovery resources in my area

List three things you can do to improve relationships within your family.

Chapter 7: Questions to Ponder

Sarah's addiction allowed us to enter systems that we had never experienced before. What systems have you encountered that were surprisingly beneficial?

If you need help and keep hitting dead ends, are you open minded about where your help can come from?

Sarah struggled with letting go and trusting others. Do you know anyone who can direct you to the support you need?

Making a list of service providers and what they offered was very helpful for us so that when a crisis occurred we could access services quickly. Make a list of service providers and their numbers who can assist you in whatever situation you're going through.

Chapter 8: Questions to Ponder

Scripture says that all who believe will still have trouble in their lives. How are you preparing your relationships now to endure trouble that will come?

Can you think of a situation that has divided your family or tested your faith?

How will you work through this?

How will you trust the Lord in your situation?

What are the things you have to let go of in order to forgive in this situation?

Chapter 9: Questions to Ponder

What old behaviors do you find difficult to overcome?

In what ways does it seem like people have given up on you?

How have you ever given up on yourself?

How can you reach out for help again?

In what ways can you support the person that has relapsed yet again?

Chapter 10: Questions to Ponder

How is your heart? What emotions have bubbled up as you read this book?

How will you process these emotions?

What spiritual nuggets will you take away and apply to your own situations?